including safeguarding-specific guidance. Leadership and managerial responsibilities are focused upon, including the key role held by the **Designated Person for Safeguarding**.

Working across the 'safeguarding spectrum'

There is specific focus in this book on the early years provider's specific safeguarding role and responsibilities within the context of having set down the aforementioned firm foundations for practice. A practical approach to safeguarding is presented and illustrated through detailed case study material – from the perspectives of legal definitions and guidance, the meaning in practical terms and what working across the **safeguarding spectrum** really means to the early years practitioner's role.

Effective intervention is considered at the **early help** stage as well as when concerns have reached a **child protection** level. A structure is presented to analyse risk, harm and need in relation to strengths and protective factors.

Across both the wider Children's Service and, where appropriate, Adults' Services, the early years practitioner's role in working effectively with other professionals is also looked at, with a guide to an accurate understanding of the **information-sharing guidance** and its relationship to confidentiality. A particular emphasis is given to the complexity of working as a member of the wider inter-disciplinary professional network, including the need to be mindful of potential hazards.

There are serious costs to children's protection and safety where practitioners fail to work together effectively, but the benefits of engaging in honest, open relationships with parents about professional concerns for them *and* their children are made explicit.

This book also underlines the responsibility of early years provisions to be constantly reflective of their practice, active in putting measures in place to minimise allegations and complaints and what must happen where they arise. The fundamental importance of teamworking is addressed, whether this is within a childminding household or group care provision, alongside guidance on designing and adopting agreed ways of working in the form of a **professional code of conduct**. This will illustrate the significance of emotional maturity or competence of the practitioner and how that will impact on work with children, their parents and members of the wider team. Where allegations

do arise against practitioners, this book provides a clear guide on the manager and registered person's legal responsibilities; including recognition, initial response and procedural steps to be taken whether an allegation is made against a childminder and/or family member or a member of a group care provision.

Lastly, this book reflects on the importance of the **leadership** role, whether this is within a childminding household or group care provision. Leaders are urged to consider the courage it takes to be a leader, including being the 'standard bearer' for high-quality child care provision. They are asked to examine the relationship between leadership, management and business ownership whilst being a 'reasonable employer', and how to care for the well-being of practitioners whilst holding practitioners to account in delivery of high standards.

With focus on the leadership role in modelling exemplary standards, leaders are encouraged throughout to adopt and fulfill a bold vision for childcare, including honest ownership of safeguarding responsibilities, evolving the development of the Designated Person for Safeguarding role and working in close partnership with them to monitor and manage the emotional competence of individual practitioners and the team as a whole.

In conclusion, this book describes an effective childcare environment as one where practitioners are consciously competent in their role and practice with confidence. This is represented by:

- Meaningful investment in continuing growth and development

- The fundamental importance of professional reflection

- Evolving a comprehensive model for being a learning provision for children, parents, practitioners, managers and the wider professional network

- Systems to support and promote the embedding of professional learning, including supervision and appraisal

- Integrating the provision's philosophy and values into recruitment and selection processes

- How early years practitioners, whether offering child care from a home or group care environment, behave in relation to children, their parents, each other within the team (including within the childminder's home) and with professionals within the wider Children's Services network.

Chapter 1

The early years practitioners team: Our biggest resource

How best can we as early years practitioners safeguard and protect young children, their families and ourselves? Two basic conclusions present themselves: there is no childcare provision without children, and there is no provision without early years practitioners. So the journey begins with us, early years practitioners. We are, in fact, our own biggest resource.

Whether you are a lone early years practitioner working from your home as a childminder, or a practitioner working within a children's centre, independent or community nursery, pre-school group, stay and play group or drop-in, you are the most precious resource. We work with young children in their most formative years and with parents (or those with parental responsibility), in supporting their child's growth and development. Our role is of vital importance. After all, the Early Years Foundation Stage is named the 'Foundation Stage' for a reason; we are playing a key part in setting down the building blocks for the rest of a child's life and for their transition into adulthood.

Working in the helping professions requires practitioners who are prepared to reflect carefully on what they bring to work every day and actively want to hone their skills to become an 'artist in human relationships'. This is especially important for working with young children as they instinctively know whether we like them or not. This heart-felt commitment to working with children

Children instinctively know if people like them

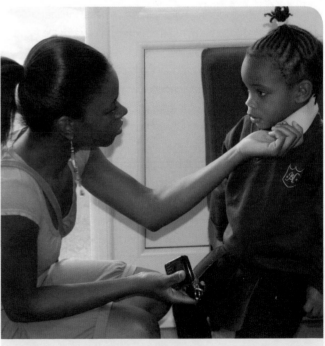
Heart-felt commitment

Safeguarding and Child Protection in the Early Years

Protecting children and their families in early years settings

Catherine Rushforth

Contents

Published by Practical Pre-School Books, A Division of MA Education Ltd, St Jude's Church, Dulwich Road, Herne Hill, London, SE24 0PB.
Tel: 020 7738 5454 www.practicalpreschoolbooks.com

© MA Education Ltd 2012

Practical Pre-School Books and the author extend their gratitude towards the parents and children of for agreeing to be involved in the photoshoot. None of the photographic images used in this book are of children or parents who are currently involved, or have ever been involved in, safeguarding or child protection investigations.

All images © MA Education Ltd., other than the images listed below:
Front cover images: (clockwise) © iStockphoto.com/YinYang, © iStockphoto.com/James Richey. All photos are taken by Lucie Carlier, with the exception of front cover (bottom right), and page 22 which were taken by Ben Suri, page 6 © iStockphoto.com/elenaleonova and page 46 © iStockphoto.com/Dmitry Merkushin

ISBN 978-1-907241-27-7

362.76

189923

Setting firm foundations for practice

How the philosophy is understood by parents

Maintain an emotionally warm physical environment

To focus on professional values and how these are expressed within the early years environment, early years practitioners and managers – whether they are home-based or work from a group care provision – need to reflect on their motivation for working in childcare and their genuine commitment to developing themselves as 'artists in human relationships'. This will involve looking closely at the ways in which their day-to-day behaviours and conduct affect children, their families and the wider team. In terms of their role in recruiting, inducting and training, they need to assess their emotional competence, including that of their colleagues and hold a deep understanding of what deems a person 'suitable' to work in childcare.

This book highlights the importance of developing a clear **philosophy** or ethos for the childcare provision, whether this is the 'feel' of the childminder's home, or a group care-setting. It prompts early years practitioners and managers to discuss and

explore their philosophy, to define and take ownership of it both verbally and in written material. They can identify the specific and practical ways in which this philosophy is expressed daily and how it is understood and experienced by children, in partnership with parents, practitioners and professionals outside the provision. This in turn, provides a clear framework to refer to when it is challenged or disregarded.

This book also examines the interface between the **Early Years Foundation Stage** (EYFS) and its application in everyday practice with children and their families. The provision's responsibilities in safeguarding children, their families and each other are explored; with emphasis on maintaining a safe, secure and emotionally warm physical environment, and 'safer' attitudes, behaviour and relationships at its heart. The systems and structures to provide stability for children are covered, with the importance of a comprehensive suite of policy and procedure, and their families is what stands between an average, okay provision and one where children are excited to go and parents are proud to say their child attends.

What is interesting to note is that child and parental opinions rarely have anything to do with the physical environment. Despite the spotlessly clean household or group care provision awash with beautiful wooden furniture and cute displays of children's wellies, it is the people we remember.

Practitioners who are warm, welcoming people, committed to the nurture, development and care of children – *those* should be the practitioners who are working with young children in their most formative years. These practitioners often possess a good supply of natural empathy and an active willingness to work *with* parents, offering support and advice where appropriate. It is in this area, however, that practitioners often feel least confident, particularly when safeguarding matters arise.

Although partnership with parents is a theme that runs throughout this book and is a discrete section within Chapter 2, there are some essential considerations as to how we can support parents in their relationship to their children from a very early stage. Central to this is the opportunity we have to see the parent and child together on a frequent basis and to notice the quality of their relationship. We are in a unique position to recognise unusual interactions between them and to pick up signals of insecure attachment. We will explore 'signals' of both secure and insecure attachment in much greater depth in Chapter 4, when we will focus on our role across the entire 'safeguarding spectrum' of work with children and their families.

A number of key reports published recently have commented on our role in this 'early help' and intervention with young children and their parents. (Allen G, 2010, Munro E, 2011, Tickell C 2011, Field F 2010). These reports, and the research on which they are based, inform us that the greatest damage to a developing infant's brain occurs during pregnancy and in the first 18 months of life (Munro E, 2011). This fact gives us ample evidence to ensure that all early years practitioners, particularly those working with babies, should be our most skilled, well-informed and competent. They should hold detailed knowledge on the importance of parent and child attachment upon the baby's developing brain and be aware of the ways in which the attachment between baby and parent can be supported and encouraged.

Attachment and the link to baby brain development

The significance of a strong bond or attachment between the baby and parent has been recognised for a long time. What has not been so clear though is the vital importance of secure attachment to the growing baby's brain development. So, what is attachment and how does it happen?

From the point of early pregnancy the initial stages of building a relationship to the unborn baby, or attachment, begin. The first images on screen at the early ultrasound are treasured moments for the vast majority of parents-to-be, as is the stage of a kicking baby in the womb. Pregnant women are often seen stroking their swelling stomach and talking to their baby. Their partners are generally supportive, already protective of their unborn child by ensuring their partner gets enough rest, good food, exercise and healthcare. In some situations though, the circumstances of the pregnancy are abusive, the baby may be unwanted and the parents' lifestyle may be inconsistent with growing a healthy baby. Examples of harm or risk towards unborn babies include smoking, use of some medications, drug or alcohol abuse, a range of self-harming behaviours and domestic abuse. In these situations, we know from research (Cleaver, H, Unell, I & Aldgate, J, in press), that the baby is already experiencing the anaesthetic effect of substances, is experiencing distress, and their developing infant brain is being damaged. For this reason, pregnant women who are harming themselves and their baby in this way often come to the attention of health and social care services, under the child protection radar for further assessment.

In the vast majority of cases, however, parents-to-be act in a responsible and mature way and eagerly await the arrival of their baby. At birth, the baby arrives pre-programmed to 'hook' the parent. This can be seen in the very early stages in the way that new-born babies gaze, staring at their parent, almost demanding that this gaze is returned – and so begins the process of 'falling in love'. This process is supported by skin-to-skin contact with the parent, identifying each other by smell and the baby having their basic needs met. In the first days of life the attachment grows stronger as the baby cries, communicating he has a need and the parent reciprocates. As this need-and-response connection becomes predictable to the baby, the sense of stability and security grows and so does the attachment. In turn, the reliable response by the parent gives rise to the baby exploring early communication; including a mirroring of facial expressions such as frowning, mouth movements, eye-crinkling and smiling. Later in development the older baby progresses to making sounds and eventually recognisable words.

Throughout this process of forming attachment between parents and baby, messages are being given and received within the baby's brain. The neurons of the brain are rapidly making connections and developing the brain for full adult capacity. At three months, the baby has more than 1,000 trillion synapses, or connections between neurons. This process will continue throughout the growing baby's childhood if the parent and other primary caregivers are well 'tuned in' to the baby in a reliable and consistent way. This fundamental emotional security for the baby enables them to develop the capacity for empathy with and for others, learning and understanding, memory and social skills.

Although relatively few practitioners will come into contact with babies under three months and witness the early attachment pattern forming between parents and baby, it is essential that they can recognise signs of an obvious and secure attachment. It is of equal importance that practitioners can identify signals of insecure attachment, a lack in parent empathy towards their baby and/or a lack of parental responsiveness or confidence. Both during babyhood and later childhood, practitioners are in a unique position to intervene, support, encourage and give advice to parents. They may be the first professional to notice that the mother may be suffering post-natal depression and to support her in receiving appropriate medical support. They may also pick

Early attachment is fundamental to brain development

up on the smallest detail that may assist in supporting the biggest difference to the relationship between the child and their parent. It is therefore essential that the practitioner is confident both in themselves and their professional capacity and is managed in such a way that they are enabled to nurture and care for children in their care, in meaningful partnership with their parents.

Although partnership with parents is a core element to providing high quality childcare, there are some essential elements to consider when reflecting on the resources of practitioners, including their skills and competencies. Practitioners need to be competent in working with children throughout their early years, responsive and supportive to work with children's parents and able to function effectively as a member of a team. In order to provide a secure framework for this vital work, attention should be given to 'safer practices' across the entire provision structure, whether this is a childminder's home or a group care setting. At the organisational and managerial levels these include safer recruitment and induction of practitioners, setting the framework for safer teamwork and ensuring practitioners are sufficiently emotionally mature to work with children during their most formative years.

Building on a framework of competency

There is extensive guidance available to guide early years practitioners in being prepared for their role to form meaningful partnership with parents in the care, nurture and development of their children. These include:

a) The Early Years Foundation Stage (DfE, 2012)

b) Common Core of Skills and Knowledge (DfE, 2010)

These set out the minimum standards for supporting children and their families.

In addition, guidance specific to early years practitioners' legal responsibilities to safeguard children and their parents is set out in:

What to do if You're Worried a Child is Being Abused (2006). *Working Together to Safeguard Children* (2010, currently under review).
Local Safeguarding Children Board policy, procedure and protocol, based on the specific needs of children and families within the local area in which the provision is located.

These guidance documents provide a framework for early years practitioners to follow in providing high standards of care for children and their families.

Whether practitioners work alone as registered childminders, or as a part of a wider team within a registered group care provision, the following should be noted. **Group care provision** – it is the responsibility of the registered person, (who may be the proprietor or owner and/or the manager), to ensure that these standards are in place. **Childminders** – they *are* the registered provider and it is therefore their responsibility to adhere to these requirements, while noting the differences as they mostly work within their own home environment. For childminders, much of the information referred to in the next two sections is discussed during their attendance on the 'Introduction to Childminding Practice' course within their home local authority. This is then tested by Ofsted at registration and subsequent inspections. Although the next two sections are primarily relevant to group care provision, there are aspects of developing safer childcare practice within the home that are relevant to childminders and/or family members.

Safer teams:
safer recruitment practice

A robust recruitment and selection process*, reflected in a clear policy for safer recruitment, is a fundamental foundation to creating a secure environment for young children and their parents. This includes explicit reference to the safeguarding element of the practitioner's role at the following stages:

- As the job is advertised

- When an application is submitted

- At interview.

It is essential that written information is matched and cross-referenced at interview stage, to ensure consistency across all forms of information, i.e. is the person being interviewed the same person who made the application? Do their personal details, qualifications and range of experience match what is written on the application form?

It is of equal importance that those included on the interview panel are suitably qualified in childcare, have attended a 'Safer Recruitment and Selection' certified course and are confident in

POINT FOR REFLECTION

Let's take a moment to reflect on who we are and the fundamental values we hold.

Remember, reflection time is a vital tool to development of a truly professional service to children and their families. It gives us (both individually and collectively), the opportunity to pause and to look at where we are, whether we are moving ahead in the direction that we really want to, including whether it is 'in step' with high quality child care and to reconsider our approach and to make changes if necessary.

Consider these statements and respond to them honestly.

- Do you and/or members of your team actively like children?

- Are you excited by the opportunity to see a child grow and develop in front of your very eyes?

- Are you enthralled by individual children's personalities, characteristics and abilities?

- Are you delighted by the opportunity you have to contribute to their development?

- Are you genuinely prepared to work in close partnership with parents, including when you need to have potentially difficult conversations with them?

- Are you energetic, enthusiastic and eager to play a part in developing children to the absolute best they can be?

- Do you celebrate all children for their unique qualities, parentage and background? Do you hold as essential celebrating diversity and anti-discriminatory ways of working?

- Can you say 'I enjoy my work'?

As a starting position, 'yes' answers to these questions will give you an idea as to whether childcare is the profession for you.

There are many other jobs and professions if the honest answer is 'no'.

probing applicants during interview. There should be a set range of questions that are asked of all applicants, which test both safeguarding knowledge towards children and their families and their responsibility to conduct themselves in a professionally appropriate way, including whistle-blowing on colleagues. This knowledge and ability to apply it to practice should be tested through presentation of a child protection scenario to all applicants. The panel should satisfy itself that the applicant is aware what safeguarding means, including early interventions with children and their families and their legal responsibility to act according to the child protection procedure.

The interview panel should employ an objective approach to assessing an applicant's suitability to the job advertised, as opposed to acting on a 'feelings level', where applicants might be liked or not. The panel members should also trust their professional opinion in judging whether the applicant appears to possess appropriate professional values for working with children and their families. For example, does the applicant demonstrate understanding of children and their parents' emotional and social development? Do they appear open, honest and emotionally mature in their attitudes? Do they refer to professional standards in their work or perhaps communicate quite fixed attitudes on how they believe children and their parents should be treated?

Prior to any firm decisions being made on whether the applicant is to be offered a job, the panel should ensure that the applicant is aware that the offer of employment is subject to satisfactory professional references, evidence of professional qualification and full enhanced CRB check with the Independent Safeguarding Authority. Thorough attention should be given to the applicant's opportunity to disclose any criminal convictions, cautions or any legal orders which may limit or disqualify them from working with children and/or vulnerable adults who are parents. It should be noted that it is an offence to employ someone who has been disqualified from working with children (Childcare Act 2006, Section 76).

It is essential that the messages from the Plymouth Serious Case Review (Plymouth Safeguarding Children Board, 2010) are fully integrated into early years provider's Safer Recruitment and Selection Policy. This serious case review gives a thorough description of the Plymouth nursery environment, leadership style, culture of team working, relationship dynamic with parents which all give a clear insight into how Vanessa George was able to sexually harm children without challenge. This report makes a number of suggestions regarding the 'characteristics of a safe setting' (addressed in Chapter 8) and refers to the importance of robust safer recruitment policy. It also reminds providers that they should not be over-reliant on good professional references and 'clear' CRB checks being an insurance that this practitioner is 'safe' to work with children. (Providing a safe environment for children and their families is explored in greater depth in Chapter 3).

The interview process should probe for emotional competence in the practitioner

Team training events provide the opportunity for honest and respectful discussion

Safer practitioners: the induction process

As the newly arrived practitioner begins work in the provision it is important that they are welcomed fully and introduced to both the unique features of this team, approach to professional practice with children and their families, and how these are reflected in the policies and procedures. A thorough induction is central to the new practitioner beginning to feel a part of the provision and to assume their position within it. The induction process* should be led by a senior early years practitioner or manager and should follow a stepped approach. The practitioner should be introduced to key policies during their first weeks within the position, rather than being overwhelmed by a huge file which they are expected to absorb by magic. This stepped approach should be reflected in an induction plan for the practitioner and, from a good human resources perspective, should be recorded by the senior practitioner or manager providing the induction. The induction process should be phased over the first months of the practitioner's arrival within the setting, keeping in step with how the practitioner is absorbing the information, and should be supported by attendance on key training courses.

It should be recognised that the wider team holds a vital role in the delivery of the induction for their colleague. They may do this in a number of ways, including:

- The way in which they model the provision's approach to practice, including the link between practice with children and their families and what the policies and procedures say

- Actively intervening in an honest and respectful way if they notice the practitioner doing or saying something that does not fit with the way they work, or the policy and procedure says they work

- Supporting the practitioner in forming relationships with children, their families and including them as a part of the team

- Providing the space for the practitioner to take up their place within the team, including the opportunity to show their own personality and contribute their own experience and skills

- Not excluding the practitioner, undermining them in their work with children and their families, gossiping about them, or, 'telling tales' on them to the manager.

In this way the practitioner can enter the team as an equal member and begin to flourish in a professionally warm and positive environment.

It should be remembered that the practitioner team is constantly being monitored and observed by children, parents, wider family members and visiting professionals alike, in an ongoing way. In a team composed of emotionally mature and professional practitioners, they would therefore take responsibility for resolving any disagreement or friction within the team. It should be noted, however, that where the team does allow frictions or splits to set in, this threatens and unsettles the emotional security for both the children and their parents. It also often creates an emotionally tense environment, where children and parents become destabilised and this places practitioners and the team as a whole in a potentially vulnerable position. This is the professional environment that could be described as emotionally abusive and neglectful, including one where complaints and/or allegations are more likely to arise.

Safer professional practice: building on emotional competence

Early years practitioners are drawn from a broad spectrum of our communities. They represent a rich diversity of ethnicity, nationality, religion, academic ability, social class, sexual orientation, age and gender. Practitioners also carry with them their own earlier life history, including both negative and positive experience. It is therefore vital to acknowledge that this will mean that some practitioners carry a history of abuse and/ or neglect from their own childhood and/or adulthood. Given current national statistics, there will be practitioners, both childminders and those working in group care provision, who are experiencing the impact of abuse and/or neglect daily or indeed, are harming others. (For example, Women's Aid (2011) report one in four women will be a victim of domestic abuse in their lifetime, many of these on a number of occasions. On average two women per week are killed by a current or former male partner). It is for this reason that it is not possible to be absolutely confident that all practitioners are 'safe' to work with children and their families. As human beings we are all a fine balance of social and emotional health and well-being every day, and it may take little to upset this balance.

In a safe early years provision where practitioners truly value themselves and their colleagues and where they do truly own that we are our biggest resource, it will be evident that they understand what this 'fine balance' really means. This would be reflected in practitioners being able to disclose their past or current circumstances in an appropriate way and to be supported. There will be some practitioners who will have worked through their own experience of childhood abuse, who can identify trigger points in their day-to-day work with children and their families and are truly reflective. These are largely practitioners who quietly and confidently share this past in a confidential and professional way. These practitioners, as they are communicative, honest and open in their approach, are generally speaking, safer in their professional practice. There are other practitioners, however, who may not have arrived at a place of 'emotional containment' of their abusive experience and who may pose a risk within a childcare environment.

A practitioner who may pose a risk in the childcare environment may come across as emotionally needy in some of the following ways:

- Lacks professional confidence, is timid and requires a great deal of support and direction in their day to day work

- Presents as overly confident, perhaps 'a rescuer', is frequently the mouthpiece for others, perhaps a 'fighter' or protagonist

- Overly confident, sharing very personal details about their life in an unbounded or 'brave' way with others, including practitioners and/or parents

- Dramatic and unpredictable, may be quite maverick or uncontained in their capacity to work with others, perhaps offers advice in an ill-considered way

- Fragile and easily upset on an emotional level or overly emotional in their work, might also avoid emotion-based discussion

- 'Cut off' and perhaps see things in quite fixed ways, especially with regard to relationships, distant and cool in an attempt to contain their emotional responses.

It should be noted that these descriptions are not intended to be understood as 'types' of practitioners, but as varying emotional 'states', which may blur the practitioner's vision in noticing the needs of children and their families.

In identifying these descriptions of behaviours, it is important to recognise that some practitioners may be in a number of

different emotional and psychological states regarding their past or current circumstances. These might include their being unaware, partially aware or fully aware of the effects of abuse and neglect on the way that they function day-to-day. This will mean that there will be childminding households and group care provision where some practitioners may be doing the following:

- Acting in a way that suggests abusive and/or neglectful behaviours are okay

- Attempting to 'heal or repair' themselves of their past abuse or neglect by placing themselves in a childcare environment

- Adopting the position of a child within the childcare environment, relating to the children as brothers and sisters and punishing them for what they did or did not receive during their own childhood

- Placing themselves in a position to be 'cared for', as if they were a child, by other caring and nurturing practitioners.

Acting from these emotional states, or playing roles such as a victim or aggressor as a practitioner within a childcare provision, obviously represents an emotional conflict of interests. The conflict that the team and management face is whether the practitioner is so absorbed in their own emotional state they are unable to fulfill their professional role in an adult, mature way towards the children and families with whom they work. The emotional state of the practitioner may be a consistent state or one that he or she slips in and out of. In both circumstances, however, it will often mean that the practitioner cannot be relied upon to be emotionally consistent in their:

- Response to children, particularly children's emotional needs

- Relationships with children's parents

- Role as an equal member of a practitioner team

- Capacity as a manager.

In such situations this practitioner poses a risk to the stability, security and safety of the childcare provision. In these circumstances it would be appropriate for the manager or external lead person for safeguarding within the local authority, to assess the practitioner's health, well-being and suitability to remain in the provision through human resources procedures. (The role of the manager in this kind of scenario is expanded further in Chapter 7.)

Example: Parent perspectives on choosing childcare

"We remember the people, not the cute displays of children's wellies"

Perceptions of what makes for a great childcare provision vary according to who is looking. These two examples are taken from new mothers who are both successful career women and were generous in sharing their views on visiting a range of childcare provision. Although they both knew they wanted children, neither had anticipated the very deep emotional bond that they formed with their baby sons. I talked with them regularly and at length, assisting them to 'quiet the chatter' in their heads about wanting to return to work, to find just the right childcare for them and to offer reassurance in readiness for the emotionally charged separation from their babies.

These brief case study examples are an opportunity for us to gain insight into how childcare provision might come across to parents, and also to highlight the significance of parents' feelings about leaving their child for the first time. This is particularly important to our broader safeguarding role as we are setting the early foundations upon which our professional relationships with parents are built. We are, after all, working in the sensitive area of human relationships and not with 'things', as you might if you worked in a

science laboratory. It is therefore vital that we are 'tuned in' to the emotional world of children, their parents and ourselves. Without this sensitive focus, our professional approach becomes mechanical and robotic.

As first-time mothers, both Audrey and Paula were embarking upon finding childcare for the first time. Neither of them had any prior experience of childcare provision themselves or any experience from which to draw in their family networks. They were both anxious about who they could trust to care for their precious babies. I talked with each of them and with their respective husbands before they began their search, while they were visiting a range of provision and at the point when they were making their final decisions.

Both looked at a range of provision. For Audrey, this included considering both childminders and nursery. Paula, following our discussions, decided that she wanted to look for a childminder. This was informed by her wish for her son to have his first formal caring experience and contacts with other children in a homely environment.

Example: Parent perspectives on choosing childcare

A child-friendly and warm environment

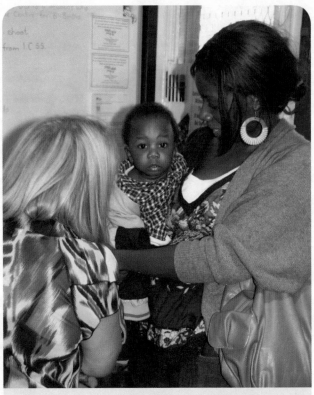

It is vital that practitioners have the ability to interact with both the parent and the child

As resourceful women they employed a number of approaches. They asked around in their local communities, went online and looked at mums.net and entered into detailed searches. They cross-referenced what was being said about respective providers online through community blogging sites and accessed Ofsted inspection reports.

Both mothers then set about making visits to providers, with their boys. I received some hilarious and some disturbing emails and telephone calls during this time. (Naturally, as Audrey, Paula and I are friends, they talked freely about their experiences and asked whether what they were experiencing, was 'normal'.)

What was very interesting, as an early years qualified professional myself, was that they both quickly commented on a number of things that were very similar. These included:

● A beautifully decorated and equipped provision, sometimes seemed a bit institutional and left them cold

● They were received in quite a formal way

● How ill at ease the practitioner seemed with selling themselves and their provision, including their unique features

● On occasion, the practitioner they were talking with made no attempt to connect with their baby

● Baby provision in nurseries was, in some cases, regimented and impersonal

● They, as the visitor, seemed to need to lead the meeting, rather than the practitioner taking more of an initiative

● Ofsted inspection judgments had little to do with their decision about who they would choose.

Audrey, who was looking at nurseries, also noted how very young some of the practitioners were. Paula also reflected that although she was very organised and tidy herself, she was made to feel uneasy by a very tidy childminder's home. She also noticed that the temperature in the home seemed to match the emotional warmth of the childminder.

Example: Parent perspectives on choosing childcare

Between them, Audrey and Paula visited in excess of twenty-five provisions before deciding on the right place for them and their sons. Although this 'snapshot' does not necessarily represent a valid, clinically analysed piece of research, it does tell us a great deal about how parents might perceive early years provision. Also, the quality and culture of this early interaction, as mentioned earlier, sets the tone for development of the parent/practitioner relationship, stretching into the future.

Both Audrey and Paula are delighted by their decisions. Audrey found a small community nursery much closer to her home than she had expected, so her son has the added benefit of being in his own community. She was completely 'won over' by the warmth of the nursery proprietor and manager, who answered the door in the midst of a crisis. She explained that she could not spend time with Audrey but she was very welcome to join the practitioners in the baby room for a brief visit.

Audrey described her hour at this nursery as 'real'. She noticed that the babies received a great deal of physical contact from the practitioners and a small toddling boy was quickly soothed by an obviously familiar adult when he toppled over. She was impressed by the amount of apparent chaos in the room, but that there were babies playing with sand, crawling in a small fenced off area of the garden and others were looking through a fence at the bigger children, accompanied by another practitioner who Audrey described as constantly chatting away. Audrey, her husband and their baby's grandma continue to be happy with the warm reception they receive in this family-run provision and their little boy is well-settled and happy.

Like Audrey, Paula visited a number of childminders before she narrowed down the 'contestants' to just two. As with Audrey, she liked the fact that the childminder she chose was friendly but professional. As a pretty strong character herself, she also had strong feelings about her childminder being confident and assertive. After all, this would be the person who might need to summon emergency help if her son was injured in any way. Paula also noticed that this childminder made a warm connection with her son from their first meeting. She did not force herself upon him, but showed him a number of toys and he quickly engaged in play, keeping an eye both on her and his mum. Paula

commented that both she and her son seemed relaxed in this household.

At this early stage Paula referred to the childminder giving a clear picture of her daily routine with the children, which children attended on different days of the week and the need for the arrangement with Paula to fit with dropping off and collecting her own children at school. They needed to negotiate the best arrangements for both parties and Paula has the added benefit that her childminder now collects her son, upon return from dropping off her own children at school.

One of the factors that influenced Paula choosing this childminder, as opposed to the other 'contender', was that she confidently asked for an opportunity to visit Paula, her husband and son in their home. She explained that she wanted to be able to picture Paula's son in his own home environment and for her husband to feel reassured that his son was being cared for by a responsible person, who he had met.

Paula's son has now been in the care of his childminder for three months and, like Audrey, she is delighted by her choice. Following the settling period, Paula called me one evening to ask if it was normal for childminders to give such extensive written feedback about her son's day. She went on to explain that her childminder had brought a small, bound notebook and had recorded nappy changes, food, her son's interaction with the other children, activities and outings during the day and the fact that he had not slept at all. At the time that Paula had collected her son, the childminder also informed her that it was not unusual for babies to not sleep in unfamiliar surroundings and suggested that Paula might bring a familiar, soft toy that he goes to bed with, the next day. This, Paula commented, worked like magic.

Paula continues to be impressed by her childminder and the gentle but assertive way that she nurtures their parent and childminder partnership in meeting the needs of her son in the best possible way.

Finally, when I approached Audrey and Paula to gain their consent to share their experiences for this book, I asked them to consider what had most influenced their final decisions – both said the warmth shown towards them *and* their boys.

LINKS WITH YOUR PRACTICE

The 'fundamental and essential' elements of warm, nurturing care towards children and their parents includes:

- How we think about ourselves as early years professionals, the standards, principles and values we hold, including how we demonstrate these to everyone who enters the provision

- Whether we are really aware of the importance of the way in which we are viewed as early years practitioners, including how we 'are' throughout the day, how we act or behave, what we say or do not say

- The ways our individual behaviour effects children in their most tender and formative years

- The significance in what we are modelling for children, their parents and for each other

- Key messages from recent publications on the link between parent: baby attachment and the baby's brain development, the essential role played by early years practitioners in identifying needs and then providing early help and intervention ourselves as professionals

- Being mindful that needy, emotionally immature adults are frequently attracted to child care, how they may distract attention onto themselves and measures to put in place to assess the practitioner's 'suitability' to child care and therefore ensure the central focus is upon the children

- Highlighting the responsibilities of the wider team, and in the case of childminders, the family, to play their part in supporting each other as a professional unit, owning their part in identifying and expressing concerns and playing their key role in solution-finding and change

- Organisational and managerial responsibilities in building and developing a professionally competent and confident team that is capable of delivering warm, nurturing care to children and their families according to policy and procedure, in a consistent and reliable way.

*Extensive guidance is available via the Department for Education and Ofsted to guide Registered Persons in development of policy and procedures. This includes:

- Safer recruitment and selection
- Induction standards
- Content for professional training in childcare.

KEY POINTS IN THE EARLY YEARS PRACTITIONERS TEAM: OUR BIGGEST RESOURCE

- It is vital to remember that as early years practitioners you are 'on stage' each and every day

- Children, parents, fellow practitioners and visiting professionals are all assessing your performance

- Make sure that your actions, behaviour, attitudes, what you say and how you say it, are 'in step' with a professional who works with children

- Your professional warmth, ability to nurture children and active enjoyment in furthering their development, really should be obvious to all

- At your most skillful you are described as 'an artist in human relationships'

Chapter 2

'Where the heart is': Developing and sticking to your philosophy

In Chapter 1, the importance of a warm, welcoming environment, where children and their families are nurtured and cared for, was stressed. In this chapter we will continue this professional journey by looking at:

- The philosophy of the child care provision and how it informs professional relationships with children, their families and fellow practitioners

- Making partnership with parents a meaningful reality

- The role of the key worker – what it does and does not involve.

Why is a philosophy important?

Safeguarding work with children and their families can be complex, particularly where professional or parent concern has reached a level that would be described as child protection. At this time emotions can run high and both relationships and communication can be put to the test. It is therefore essential to be confident about the philosophy you have in place for your child care provision. This philosophy will guide:

- The foundations upon which relationships are formed and maintained

- The tone for communication

- Expectations for the way in which all professional practitioners conduct themselves in relation to children, their parents, wider family, each other within the practitioner team and members from the broader professional network

Is it explicit in your setting that children are the central focus?

- A framework for resolving upsets, disputes and complaints.

The provision philosophy provides the 'touchstone' upon which to check that you are working in a consistent way. It leads you back to your fundamental values, beliefs and principles and reminds you of the reasons for doing what you do, in the way that you do it.

What is your philosophy?

Although child care provision, including childminders and the full range of group care, is registered under the Early Years Foundation Stage, the different kinds of provision are hugely diverse. There are some which are known for their religious principles, some for their exciting outside Forest School facilities and some that are closely affiliated with particular primary schools, including independent schools. Some childminders speak several languages or specialise in the care of very young babies. So, there is the 'what' you provide that might be especially unique and then there is the 'how' you provide it. This will be informed by the philosophy or ethos of the provision.

If we are to agree that our role in the helping professions is to be skillful artists in human relationships, then our core focus will be on how we do this. This is, after all, the foundation upon which high quality child care is based and is fundamental to safeguarding children, their families and practitioners. What this might include is explored below.

- Within group care provision the quality of relationship established between the proprietor, the Registered Person and the manager and their agreement about 'the way we do things here' essentially sets the tone for all other relationships within the provision and informs the philosophy. In the same way a childminding household will have their own ground rules for the home during the hours of childminding. These will be agreed between members of the household, including the childminder's partner, children (both under and over 18 years) and members of the wider family, friend and community network

- The Registered Person, whether the manager of a group care provision or registered childminder actively owning their leadership responsibilities and being fully accountable for everything that happens in their provision or home

- Ensuring that the values and principles held by the provision are translated into all written material such as the advertisements for new practitioners, the prospectus or information for parents and the full suite of policies and procedures

- What practitioners 'do' on a day-to-day basis, is a direct reflection of what the policies and procedures say they do

- Practitioners or, in the childminder's case, family members, actively question and challenge each other in making sure that the provision's values and principles (or philosophy) are followed

- Practitioners within all provisions regularly reflect on whether their philosophy might have evolved or changed and if so,

that they recognise that this has happened and adopt these changed practices across the entire team (or household) or choose not to.

How to test your provision's philosophy

As detailed, the provision's philosophy should be something that is shared across the entire practitioner team (or household) and is explicitly understood when parents choose you.

Take a few moments, preferably as a team, to conduct an assessment on how well your philosophy might be embedded.

1. Are children truly at the centre of everything you do?

   Consider whether practitioners are there for the children, or for some other reason? Do practitioners contain their emotions and conduct themselves in a professional way around the children? What informs their conduct?

2. Do parents understand your approach to their child's care and education?

   Consider whether they are aware of your philosophy, values and principles and that they chose these when they decided to register their child at your provision.

3. Do you seek regular opportunities to share development of the provision with parents?

   Consider whether you have arranged brief workshop for parents on the updating of your safeguarding policy in light of the findings of the Plymouth Serious Case Review. Are parents aware about changes to the use of mobile phones and cameras within the provision and why you ask them not to use their mobile phone within the premises?

4. Are all members of your practitioner team or household familiar with your philosophy, values and principles?

   Consider whether this includes all members of your family or, for group care provision, all members of your support team (cook, premises officer, administrative officer), early years practitioners, management committee, manager, proprietor.

5. Are all of your team members, regardless of their role or

designation, able to translate your philosophy, values and principles into day-to-day practice?

Consider whether they are able to explain what they are doing and why they are doing it in this way.

6. Are your philosophy, values and principles reflected in all of your policies and procedures?

Consider whether everyone does what your policies and procedures say you do in a consistent way.

7. Is your whole team actively willing to explain, or even defend, your values and principles when they are challenged or questioned?

Consider whether any member of your team or household could talk confidently with an Ofsted Inspector.

8. Are practitioners willing to question and challenge, even where this might make them unpopular?

Consider whether practitioners regularly enter into potentially difficult conversations with parents or each other within the team.

Does everyone have the confidence to do this?

When reflecting on these questions it is helpful to consider:

● What you are really proud of

● What is really important to you:
   In your work with children?
   In your work with parents?
   In your work as a team?

● What would suck the life out of your provision and make you feel devastated by its loss?

This exercise will almost certainly assist you in refining what you really believe in as a team or childminding household.

Remember we are playing a part in raising the next generation of parents, scientists, doctors, early years practitioners and politicians.

Be bold! Children deserve our very best!

A final note on philosophy

There are some essential elements to your philosophy in providing effective care for children and their parents.

These are:

● Children being at the heart of everything

● Honest and open relationships with parents and family members

● Teamwork, whether this is within a group care environment or home-based care.

In a successful provision there is reliable and consistent attention to high standards across all three of the above, and anyone looking in would be able to observe tangible examples to support the view that the philosophy is truly owned. It is important to remember, however, that the standards for your provision are only ever as good as the person delivering the lowest standards.

Partnership with parents

The Early Years Foundation Stage is referred to as 'the foundation' for a number of reasons. Among them is the unique opportunity that early years provision has to set the blueprint for relationship between parents and professional practitioners. The quality and effectiveness of this first relationship, which may span over the most influential and formative of the child's first four years, can set the benchmark for parents, potentially for the rest of the child's life.

Consider what this could mean. Imagine what services for children could look like if you, right from the very beginning, created honest and open relationships with parents.

Imagine that up and down the country, practitioners were building on their relationship of trust with parents by talking openly to parents about their safeguarding, including child protection, responsibilities. Imagine that they supported these conversations by providing brief workshops to assist parents in understanding stages in their child's development, how they can promote it and ways to keep their children safe.

How might these parents present themselves as they go to register their child for school?

(This section continues on page 20)

Example: Reflecting on your core values in a nursery

Learning as a whole provision community

Recognising and owning your unique qualities

Stars of Hope Nursery is located within a community centre in a busy, urban environment in South East London. The philosophy for the provision was originally based on Christian values held by the proprietor. These have been built on by her daughter, the current manager, who describes her beliefs as more spiritual. The service offered to local families has developed over the last years into a truly 'wrap around', holistic service committed to promoting the welfare and well-being of children. It is clear that both the manager and her deputy are in step with the principles of the safeguarding legislation and are cutting edge in their attention to keep evolving as a team.

The unique quality of this provision is the emphasis given to children actively experiencing respect, security, support and being loved for who they are. A particular focus is given to supporting children to develop a strong sense of themselves and their unique racial heritage, ethnicity, culture and identity. This has been a whole team endeavor,

although the early stages of the journey involved the management team challenging themselves and their team in addressing their own assumptions, myths and prejudices. There had been a simplistic view for example, that, because the children and the staff were mostly black, cultural diversity was naturally embraced. Upon closer examination, however, it came to light that few practitioners had a real sense of the children's actual heritage. This set the team on a path to actively enquire of parents as to their respective racial heritage, ethnicity, culture, religion and identity and to support learning for the children, in an active partnership.

This learning as a whole provision community is particularly important as it is also an area where young black men (including those from loving, secure families), are frequently associated with gangs, in search of a sense of identity and belonging. There is no question that the desire to instill a sense of pride, self esteem and assurance in children, by this inspiring, innovative and progressive team of practitioners is an identifying feature of their provision. It is also the very reason that a number of parents choose Stars of Hope as the nursery for their child.

Example: Childminders need to 'own' their philosophy

Opportunity for children to be part of a social group

Emphasising the benefits of group care within a home environment

In a similar vein, Christine is a registered childminder in the same London borough as Stars of Hope Nursery. She has taken time to define her philosophy and approach to work with children and their families. She has two minded children between 2-3 years old with her during the day, two children at secondary school of her own and cares for two children after school.

Christine is clear about the value she provides for children and their families within her lively, chatty and busy household. When she meets prospective parents she takes care to emphasise the benefits of what she offers as:

- Group care within a home environment; opportunity for children to be a part of a social group, where they learn to care for and be cared for, by other children under her watchful supervision

- Exposure to being a part of a group at differing stages of development, where language, self-care skills, and co-operation are modeled by other children as well as her, the adult

- Getting familiarity by frequently visiting the school environment

She also takes the time to talk with parents about what they are looking for in a childminder and carefully explains what she is and is not able to provide. For example, she believes that she is able to offer a limited amount of individual attention, particularly through the latter part of the day. She takes time to explain in detail to parents that if they are looking for a childminder who will negotiate with their child for twenty minutes to put their shoes on, that this will not work with their busy routine, including getting off to collect children at the end of the day. In short, Christine has found a way to describe her child care approach to parents, is aware of the value she provides and is not afraid to suggest to parents that she may not be the right childminder for them. In this way the very beginning of the relationship with parents is set on firm foundations, with their expectations of each other clearly agreed. Christine has also learned from experience that unmet expectations for parents often leads to 'niggles' in their relationship, upsets and on occasion, complaints.

- Might they actively enquire about the school's philosophy as they consider whether this is the right school for their child?

- Might they ask to meet the Designated Person for Safeguarding within the school and request the school procedures?

- Might they ask for guidance on what they should do if they have a suspicion that a member of the team is harming their child, as in the case of the recent teacher within the Weston-super-Mare primary school?

This might seem like a dream, but it is one that can be made a reality if you begin today. In just four years' time many more parents up and down the country could be asking confident questions and presenting themselves as full and equal partners with school teams, for the rest of their child's education.

- How could early years practitioners contribute to making this dream a reality?

- Exactly what kind of partnership would you be establishing with children's parents right now, within the early years provision, to make your relationship a truly meaningful one?

- How can it be so well established that it is set as a blueprint for parent/professional relationships for the rest of their child's life?

Recognising the child's key family member network is essential

As indicated in earlier sections of this chapter, creating a meaningful relationship with parents begins with you being clear, open and honest. This will include clarity about your philosophy or approach and honesty about what your provision can and can not provide, (as in Christine's case example). It will also entail giving careful thought to the following:

- Ensuring that your discussions with the parent/s are a truly two-way process. This involves being responsible for recognising the amount of power you hold, owning your professional expertise, knowledge and skills while also asking key questions of the parent, as the expert on their relationship and knowledge of their child.

- Being friendly, warm and open in your interaction with the parent, but not giving the impression that you intend to be their friend or that you will bow under any inappropriate influence they might apply. It should be recognised that establishing clear professional boundaries within the parent/practitioner relationship is a delicate balance, but the responsibility for setting and maintaining the boundary lies with the practitioner.

- Paying attention to the way that the parent comes across in their interaction with you throughout the stages of your relationship. Your observations are valid and should guide you in how you carry on with the parent on a day-to-day basis. For example, while it might be fairly usual for some parents to be anxious, a little defensive, or ill-at-ease in your company in the early stages of your relationship, a continued pattern of these responses should lead you to enquire as to what might be concerning the parent. This might include you reflecting on whether the parent's behaviour towards you might be related to a mental health need or learning disability, for example.

- Recognising that it may be a real emotional challenge for the parent to leave their precious child in your care, however much they have grown to trust you and whether or not they really enjoy their studies at college, or their work.

- Being mindful to maintain frequent person-to-person contact with parents of young children, ideally on a daily basis. In this way, small but often significant steps in the child's daily experience are shared and actively demonstrate the importance placed on the child as the central interest. Maintaining regular, open contact with each other should also be focused around the parent's specific needs and wishes. For example, email contact might keep the lines of communication open for a parent who is working long shifts and talking in the parent's preferred language might be essential for the delivery of key information.

- Establishing occasions for more detailed conversation with parents, to explore their child's development, well-being, progress and learning, as well as to highlight any ways in which the parent/practitioner partnership can be strengthened in support of the child. This is particularly important both for busy parents who quite literally run in and out with their child and to ensure that any needs for the child or parent, including any 'niggles' or disagreements in your relationship, are resolved at the earliest opportunity.

- Introducing the provision's policies and procedures to parents from the outset of the relationship. This, along aside inviting the parent to spend time with you beyond the initial 'settling in' period, assists the parent in understanding their child's day, including the daily routine and the way that this interfaces with your policies. Ideally, talking through the policies and procedures with parents should be in a measured, incremental way over time, rather than bombarding them with huge amounts of information at the early stages of relationship building. It is, however, essential to discuss some key policies at an early stage, in order that parents experience an honest and open dialogue with you. The provision's safeguarding policy should fall into this category and discussion with the parent should include what you do in situations when you have concerns for either the parent's or child's protection, safety, welfare and/or well-being.

- Showing sensitivity towards parents in sharing of more private or confidential information. For example, opening early conversation about your observations on a child's progress being a little delayed or indicating signs of a specific need, would be more appropriately discussed in a quiet area of the provision, or even in a separate room. In this way both the parent's needs and reactions are being considered and their right to express these in a private, confidential place, respected.

- Emphasising with parents that you will never intentionally compete with them for their child's affections and that, although children often form strong bonds with practitioners, you truly appreciate the special attachment between parent and child.

- Agreeing with the parent how they would like key, significant milestones in their child's development, including the 'golden moments' of first words or steps, shared with them. This is

LINKS WITH YOUR PRACTICE

The significance of the provision's professional philosophy, or approach to child care includes:

- The importance of the Registered Person (whether for group or home-based child care) holding a clear vision regarding the philosophy, ensuring that practitioners (or family members) share this vision and play their part in owning it

- How a shared philosophy sets the tone for everything that happens within the provision, including how it is done and as a consequence provides a firm foundation upon which all can rely, feel stable and secure

- Ensuring a consistency between policy, procedures and day to day practice in a way that is obvious and recognisable to children, parents, practitioners, professionals with whom the provision's practitioners work and Ofsted (This may have included entering into an exercise as a team to test whether everyone is 'in step' with each other)

- Recognising that the provision's philosophy should include clear references to high standards, principles and values, particularly when working in meaningful partnership with parents, where honest, open and regular dialogue is 'normal'

- Owning the professional responsibility to establish and maintain boundaries in relationships with children and their families and is friendly in their approach, whilst never seeking to become a personal friend

- Noting that setting up this kind of approach to child care means that parents can grow to trust their child's key worker as well as other practitioners within the provision and as a consequence, feel more comfortable with practitioner's enquiries when safeguarding, including child protection concerns, arise

- Considering that you are also forming the 'blueprint' for the parent's expectations (and confidence) for professional practitioner partnership throughout their child's life. In addition, it models for the child that those around them can be relied upon to provide security and safety.

POINT FOR REFLECTION

Practitioner team reflections on linking philosophy with practice

The Aylesbury Early Years Centre practitioner team has worked together over a number of years. I asked them how they had evolved their practice over the years. They told me that they have designed and refined a professional code of practice and continue to 'tweak' it as they recognise any loopholes.

Here are a few things that they had to say:

"It's about owning and wearing the cap – you cannot work with children if you do not (professionally) love them."

"Everyone here is a parent (all practitioners), we pass children's parents in the street, we all have problems, I always start from here (pointing at heart)."

"We know what professionalism is, we know what the expectations are and we do it."

"We talk with parents all the time, we don't avoid anything."

"It's our job to be emotionally literate and to provide this for children. Children greet each other in the morning. If they see we are sad, we talk about it."

"We have a culture of sharing – we communicate everything. We are different (as practitioners), but we aim to make everyone welcome."

And from the management team:

"We name the problem, then move quickly to solution – finding."

"We do praise our staff – our aim is to empower, instill trust and confidence."

"It's not what you say, it's how you say it. If it's not sincere, I don't say it, whoever it is."

From these brief quotes, you will get a sense of the provision philosophy, the culture within which they conduct themselves and the commitment shared by the team. This is what all child care provision should be creating, as a priority.

a significant consideration as practitioners are often the first to notice the final stages before the first independent step is taken and may even be the first to witness it. For parents, however, these are truly precious moments. An enthusiastic, bubbly practitioner, who shares that first step, might not have considered that a parent might feel resentful towards them for 'stealing' a special memory. In many provisions this attention to the fine detail in their relationship with parents is managed very sensitively, and although they have seen the first independent steps for the child, choose to not say anything, but suggest to the parent the moment does not seem far off.

As skillful artists in human relationships, it is important for practitioners to own their responsibility for nurturing the relationship with children's parents. Relationship-forming is a gradual, steady process that requires attention to each of the aspects detailed above. It also requires the practitioner to be focused on each parent as unique, with their own personality, characteristics, interests and needs, exactly as they do towards each unique child. Appreciation of these differences provides access to engaging with parents on an individual basis, while ensuring consistency and engagement with all parents within the provision. This amounts to a true equality in the 'partnership'.

Developing Key Person relationships

All the principles outlined in the earlier part of this chapter apply when entering into the Key Person role with a child and their parent. Particular emphasis would obviously be given to the much more personalised level of relationship within the context of a close parent/practitioner partnership. As outlined in Chapter 1, the young child's brain develops at a rapid rate when they feel both emotionally and physically safe and secure. It is therefore the primary responsibility of the Key Person to provide a reliable and consistent attachment figure for the child and a special relationship to the parent.

Mapping out the relationship between you, the Key Person, and the parent is a matter of great importance for both the child and their parent. The Key Person will focus on the specific likes and dislikes of the child, get to know how they operate as a unique little character, their strengths and anxieties. The Key Person should also develop their understanding of the child's needs around food, sleep and comfort and will get to know how to soothe the child when distressed, through detailed discussion with the parent.

Practitioners will naturally bring their professional child care experience to bear and often offer gentle advice or suggestions to the parent in forming a consistent approach to the child between home and the provision. As the Key Person is also a central attachment figure to the child, focused on all elements of their progression and well-being, in addition to actively promoting partnership with the parent, all interactions and observations made in the course of their professional role will be formally recorded.

Over time a mutual respect and appreciation between the Key Person and parent should grow and the relationship naturally deepens. As with all professionals within the helping services, however, there are potential 'emotional hazards' to consider when entering into relationships with parents. These are most successfully contained when Key Persons work within their provision's Code of Professional Conduct and maintain a consistently reflective approach to their work. It is the responsibility of the provision manager to lead, model and nurture practitioners in the development of their capacity to respond appropriately to challenging experiences with parents and to encourage emotionally mature, professional relationships.

At a basic level, it is important for all Key Persons to recognise that the parent and child have a right to receive a high standard of child care and there should be no need for the parent to reassure, praise or thank them for doing their job. It is usual however, as the partnership between parent and Key Person grows for the parent to express their gratitude, as their child shows obvious signs of being happy, safe and thriving within the provision.

It is also important for the parent and Key Person to be open to relationship with other practitioners within the provision, as opposed to nurturing an exclusive, dependent interaction. This acts as a safeguard for both the practitioner and parent in ensuring that high standards of professional conduct are observed within this relationship.

Developing as a skillful artist in human relationships is a complex process and on occasion Key Persons may cross the line and become over-involved. For example, an over-friendly relationship between a parent and Key Person may be reflected in a practitioner seeing the parent and child outside of the provision, babysits, attends their key child's birthday party or offers additional emotional or practical support 'out-of-hours'. This represents a breach of an appropriate professional boundary. Such signals of over-involvement should be challenged, whether within a home-based or group care provision. 'Looking out' for Key Persons in this way is one of the most effective safeguards to the Key Person, child and the parent.

Observation is essential to understanding the individual needs and character of each child

KEY POINTS IN 'WHERE THE HEART IS': DEVELOPING AND STICKING TO YOUR PHILOSOPHY

A clear vision and philosophy for the provision's approach to child care guides what you do and how you do it. The registered person's responsibility is to ensure that this is consistently applied in:

- How the provision is described by practitioners, parents and visiting professionals alike

- Recognition of why the parent chose the provision, in preference to another

- 'Owning' the way in which 'things are done here'

- The manner in which relationships are established and then maintained, between all parties, with particular emphasis on partnership with parents...whether this is a home-based or group care provision

Chapter 3

Creating an effective interface between policy and practice

In Chapters 1 and 2, you will have noticed the significant emphasis placed on an emotionally warm, safe and secure environment for children. In my view there is no negotiation on providing these basics for children and their families and there is little investment made by either children or parents in relationship-building or learning where these essential foundation stones are missing. As we move into a new era in childcare, focused on 'early help' (Munro, E 2011) and effective early intervention with children and their families, in my opinion we will not survive and succeed unless we embrace these principles. Children and their families deserve these as their very basic human right.

Having explored the vital importance of providing a warm, nurturing and caring environment for children and their families in this section, we will continue our journey by recognising that everything within the early years provision relates to safeguarding children, their families and each other as practitioners, in some way or another. A comprehensive approach to safeguarding therefore needs to be taken, ensuring that the EYFS Safeguarding and Welfare Requirements are fully embedded in the way the provision operates on a day-to-day basis. We shall focus on these under the following categories:

- Physical environment

- Systems and structures

- Leadership processes and organisation

- Designated or Lead Person for Safeguarding

- 'Safer' attitudes, behaviour and relationships.

Providing a safe environment for children

Ensuring that the EYFS Safeguarding and Welfare Requirements are followed within the provision is made a legal responsibility by the Childcare Act 2006.

This includes the way in which the physical space is used within the provision, how practitioners are recruited, trained and deployed, ensuring that an effective range of policies is in place to guide the approach and standards for childcare practice and that a basic routine structures the day.

Physical environment

The early years environment, whether a home setting or group care provision, needs to be fit for purpose and managed with both safety and safeguarding principles in mind. This includes:

- Being mindful of the security of the building, basic health and safety principles, an hygienic, pleasant, warm and comfortable place to be for children and their families

- Having a clear procedure in place and followed for signing children and practitioners in and out of the building, and a collection policy, with arrangements for adults (other than those originally identified as 'familiar' to children) for the collection of children

- Having access arrangements into the building monitored by practitioners and agreement established as to who opens the door and to whom

- Ensuring all visitors to the provision are formally signed in and out, irrespective of their relationship to the practitioners, children and/or parents

- Making sure that a standard practice for challenging all 'unknown' persons in the building is adopted by all practitioners

- Practitioners, children and their parents are familiar with fire evacuation procedures, as they are exercised regularly

- Risk assessment is recognised by all practitioners as their responsibility, within the building, in any outside play areas and while out on trips

- For group care provision, making sure that practitioners only work alone, in secluded parts of the building with children or vulnerable parents on rare occasions. These periods are for a specific purpose and are known to other practitioners, including an estimation as to how long the practitioner is likely to be away from the main group environment

- There is a clear policy regarding use of mobile phones and digital recording equipment. This is observed by practitioners, parents and visitors. (Like all policies within the provision, this should be clearly embedded into day-to-day practice.)

A case study to demonstrate this is included in Chapter 8.

- Practitioners are deployed within the building and outside areas according to appropriate practitioner to child ratios and individual children's specific needs

- An exciting, engaging and varied play environment is provided for children

- Open, honest and professional communication is recognised as the cornerstone to all relationships, whether with children, their parents, each other within the practitioner team (or home for childminders) and with members of the wider professional network

- Practitioners are alert to what they see, hear and feel within the environment, anticipate risks or challenges and intervene at the earliest opportunity.

Systems and structures

The suite of policy and procedure, daily routine and structures for record-keeping within the provision provides a framework for maintaining standards and consistent practice.

The basic daily routine provides a reliable pattern to the children's day and assists them in understanding the sequence

Practitioners and parents share responsibility for signing in and out of the building

Policies and procedures should be easily accessible and explanation offered to assist understanding

All practitioners share responsibility for the protection of children within the building

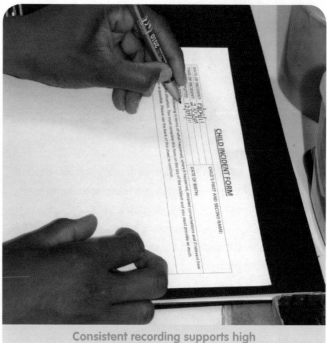

Consistent recording supports high standards in safeguarding practice

of events, boundaries in how to conduct themselves and a secure base from which to explore. A small child's experience of Grandma bringing them to the childminder's house, followed by breakfast and then dropping the big children to school before going to pre-school, offers reassurance and builds on the development of social interaction in different environments. The end-of-day routine, including collection of the big children from school, then tea and singing after tea-time, similarly offers the sure knowledge that soon their parent will come. This repeating pattern offers stability and security, where trust grows in familiar adults and children can develop their independence.

A comprehensive suite of policies and procedures also provides the framework for practitioners to deliver consistent, reliable and high quality child care, according to both generally held values in the child care profession and individual provision philosophy. These need to be supported by robust recording systems, which provide the evidence that X happened at Y time, performed by Z, on W, in a reliable way. As all individual practitioners are legally accountable for what they do or do not do (Children Act, 2004), it is essential that they are able to refer back to an instance several days, weeks, or even years later and to explain why they did X to W in the way that they did, to evidence their practice.

For example, the provision's behaviour policy should be familiar to all parents and practitioners, who should understand what it means in day-to-day practice terms. It is fully supported

by practitioners attending courses on modern methods of responding to a range of behaviours in children. Equally, this behaviour policy, written and adopted by the Willows Pre-School, for example, should be followed in a consistent way by the full team. Deviating from the behaviour policy on the other hand, where a practitioner smacks a child in their care, is a clear abuse of their professional position of trust and is a physical abuse to the child. Such an incident would be referred to Children's Social Care to consider for full investigation under child protection procedures, prior to the formal disciplinary process being followed. All policy and procedure followed within the provision should be:

1. Tailored according to the specific needs of the provision, including the children and families that access it

2. Owned by the Registered Person, manager and/or management committee as the 'Willows Pre-School approach', for example

3. Adopted by the full team

4. Formally supported by training and professional development opportunities

5. Reviewed on a frequent basis, to ensure that it sits within current and modern childcare approaches (for example, the use of 'time out' for children, used on an incremental scale

of strategies, is no longer viewed as an appropriate early intervention, but as a final response).

As indicated earlier in this chapter, the provision's policies and procedures provide the framework for day-to-day practice. Taken as a full suite of policies, they should link to each other and provide a comprehensive approach on how things are done within this group care provision or childminding household. They each have a potential relationship to safeguarding, including circumstances in which the practitioner might need to act on child protection concerns (as demonstrated in the example about the provision's behaviour policy).

Although not an exhaustive list, the range of policy and procedure within the provision should include:

- Accidents and incidents, including clear communication of information where the child has been injured either at home or in the provision

- Behaviour policy, including detailed recording of observed patterns, successful and unsuccessful ways of responding and a clear strategy agreed with parents, as appropriate

- Intimate care and nappy-changing policy, including active attention to gaining the child's agreement to be changed and care given to protecting their privacy and dignity. Equally this policy should outline the area in which children are changed and wider practitioner team awareness of where their colleagues are and for how long

- Inclusion and diversity policy, including focus on individual needs and honour of the 'unique child' and their family, active regard and respect for the rich diversity of background and belief within the provision's community

- Lost child procedure, including what practitioners should do, who to inform and when, and a follow up process that builds on professional learning as a result of the incident

- Late collection of children policy should include sensitivity towards parents' managing the demands of a hectic home/ work schedule, while also providing a clear framework for response where late collection has become persistent. As with all other policy guidance, this procedure should address the child's needs as the central focus, including measures to minimise distress to the child. This policy should address making contact with emergency back-up carers for the family

and should include adults 'known' to the child. This procedure should also offer clarity of response where the child might appear to have been abandoned and therefore require referral to Children's Social Care as a child protection matter

- The management of infection, ill children and medication policies should include a coherent approach to these closely related aspects of child care practice. They should inform a clear, consistent and caring guidance for practitioners to ensure that children's needs are held as the central focus and parents and practitioners do not inadvertently neglect the child's needs

- Complaints policy should emphasise the right of the parent to express their views regarding the quality and consistency of service offered to both themselves and their child. It should provide an easy-to-follow process for parents and for the provision to respond at both informal and formal stages

- Critical incidents policy should provide process steps for responding to an array of possible incidents that present as 'out of the ordinary' events within the provision. As with a number of other policies, it should provide guidance as to how professional learning from the incident will be integrated into review of practice to prevent or minimise such incidents arising in the future.

Although it should be noted that policies and procedures are designed to guide what practitioners do in certain everyday situations and how they do it, they should not be so rigidly applied that the care of the child becomes secondary. For example, a sleep policy might guide a general routine for toddlers to take a rest or sleep after lunch. If a child is alert and lively however, it would seem that the child does not need sleep at that time, in which case their individual needs should be honoured. On the other hand a practitioner attempting to force this child to sleep, including restraining them on a sleep mat, would be an abuse of their freedom to play and a physical abuse.

Safeguarding specific policy and procedure

Within the comprehensive range of policy and procedure to support high standards in child care, sits safeguarding specific policy and procedure. This includes the practitioner's responsibilities to respond to children and their parent's needs across the full spectrum of need from early intervention, through to targeted levels of support and, if appropriate, making a referral to Children's Social Care, where professional concern is of a child protection nature.

This policy should be supported by clear procedure, including:

- A safeguarding policy, which refers to the practitioner's role across the safeguarding spectrum, arrangements for working within the Local Safeguarding Children's Board's protocols where concerns have reached a child protection level and the role of the Lead or Designated Person for Safeguarding within the provision

- The child protection procedure which lays down the process to be followed when seeking advice and guidance from Children's Social Care and/or making a formal referral; the telephone numbers for contacting this service according to the child's home address and expectation of the way in which the Key Person and Designated Person would talk with the parent (including specific guidance to address occasions that this would not be appropriate) and when this should happen

- A code of professional conduct to guide practitioner interaction with children, their parents, each other within the team in a group care provision and with the wider family unit within a home environment. This code should also guide expectation as to what practitioners do and do not do in the course of their professional role, both while they are working and outside work hours. (This aspect of practice is examined in detail in Chapter 6.)

- A whistle-blowing policy for use by practitioners who have concern for the conduct and behaviour of their work colleagues

- A procedure to inform practice when an allegation is made against a practitioner or manager, or in the home setting, allegations against childminders and/or family members.

In conclusion, a comprehensive suite of policy and procedure works hand-in-hand with what practitioners do every day and the way in which they do it. The daily routine then sets the rhythm for the day to ensure basic care needs, including food, sleep and personal care, are given priority alongside planned opportunities for focus on learning and development through play. Taken together, these provide a consistent framework for the provision and for practitioners who work within it, to be held to account for their professional practice.

Let's pause for a moment to consider some of the key lessons from the Plymouth Serious Case Review on Z Nursery. This was a nursery in which the framework for both safety and safeguarding was inconsistent and, in parts, completely missing.

POINT FOR REFLECTION

Messages from the Plymouth Serious Case Review

A combination of factors contributed to the unsafe environment in which Vanessa George, (referred to as 'K' in the Review), could sexually abuse children in her care, unchallenged.

- Z nursery, as it is referred to in the report, was a not-for-profit organisation, jointly managed by a board of four trustees. These trustees were unaware of their responsibilities as the collective Registered Person and one trustee had died. Although Ofsted recognised the nursery manager as one of the trustees the manager disputed this. *The very foundations of the provision were therefore shaky.*

- There were no records of a job advertisement, interview or references for K. The nursery manager had been a governor at the school in which Z nursery was partially located, she got to know K through this route and sought a 'reference' from the class teacher with whom K had worked. K did have a cleared CRB check. *Recruitment and selection was based on word-of-mouth, was naïve and lacked rigour.*

- The nursery's safeguarding policy had not been formally adopted or tailored to Z nursery. Child protection procedure was not followed for fear of reprisal by parents. *The EYFS Welfare Requirements 2008, including the legal duty to safeguard children, were disregarded.*

- Although K did not hold a senior position within the nursery, her personality, age and length of service seemed to create an illusion of her holding power. When she began talking in a sexualised way within the team this illusion seemed to inhibit colleagues challenging her. *K had effectively groomed them to the point where they were silenced.*

- K deviated from the nursery's nappy changing protocol. *No-one had the confidence to challenge her.*

Learning from this SCR is explored in Chapter 6.

A consistent, nurturing care of children is central to the link between policy and practice

Effective leaders lead by example

Leadership processes and organisation of the provision

As detailed in Chapter 2, the Registered Person holds the responsibility to ensure that the provision functions in a smooth way and according to the EYFS Safeguarding and Welfare Requirements. In the case of child care offered within the home environment, the childminder holds the Registered Person status. Within the group care provision the Registered Person role may be held by the provision manager or by a person not physically involved in the day-to-day operation. In this case it is their responsibility to ensure that a competent manager is appointed to provide confident leadership to the practitioner team. This manager is accountable for addressing safeguarding standards in the following areas:

- Safer recruitment and selection of practitioners, including CRB checks at an enhanced level, Independent Safeguarding Authority vetting and barring checks and receipt of professional qualifications and references. The manager should ensure that the same principles are applied when arranging temporary agency practitioners via a reputable recruitment service, providing placements for trainees and students, offering work experience for school children and volunteers, including parents or wider family members.

- Ensuring that a thorough practitioner induction and training programme is designed and implemented for the provision. This would follow the principles of an incremental build on practitioner competence, based on the manager's assessment of each practitioner's knowledge and skills, demonstrated in the course of their work. A detailed strategy should also be in place for all practitioners to receive training in their safeguarding responsibilities, including child protection. Such courses should address their role in recognising and responding to colleagues who might harm or abuse children or vulnerable parents, their duty to whistle-blow and the allegations against practitioners' procedure. Training of practitioners in safeguarding and child protection should be provided at intervals of two-three years at a minimum and, specifically where key changes to the legislation occur, or local or provision failures to safeguard and protect children and/or their parents, come to light.

- Organising deployment of practitioners according to the needs of children and their families, on a day-to-day basis. This includes the manager basing their decisions on deployment of practitioners according to their demonstrated competence, (For instance, a practitioner who holds a level 3 qualification, but who is not able to work in an independent, responsible, consistent and reliable way, should not be entrusted with the full range of responsibilities generally associated with this role. Working within a competency framework will be explored in greater detail in Chapter 8). Child to practitioner ratios should be adhered to and overall responsibility to safeguard and protect the children within the provision should inform managerial decision-making at all times.

- Ensuring that an effective Key Person system is in place for all children within the provision. This includes the manager facilitating development of the relationship between the Key Person and the parent in their shared responsibility towards the child, making sure to deploy practitioners within the provision in such a way that this key attachment relationship is disrupted as little as possible and providing professional supervision to the practitioner in supporting the development of the Key Person role with *this* child and parent.

- Providing a reliable and accessible 'on the ground' level of daily supervision, guidance and leadership to the practitioner team, including acting as a role model for the delivery of high standards in child care practice. A formal structure for practitioner supervision and appraisal should also be in place, supported by a formal supervision policy, written agreements and action plans to provide for incremental learning and development. High value should be placed on the importance of professional reflection and opportunity for individual progression offered through supervision, including 'containment' of practitioner's emotional responses to child protection matters.

- Facilitating scheduled time for practitioner teams and individual practitioners to plan for the early year's curriculum, devising plans to promote individual children's development, or taking time out to prepare for a specific event. Examples might include organising observations of a child with view to opening a particularly sensitive discussion with a parent or preparation of a report for a child protection conference.

- Ensuring that all supporting documentation within the provision is up-to-date, of a high standard, reflects an accurate picture of discussions, events or observations, is presented in a legible form and is signed. With regard to safeguarding and child protection, records should distinguish between factual information and professional opinion, assessment and analysis and demonstrate awareness as to who might read them, including the child's parents. In a similar vein, all 'standard' records within the provision should focus in the same way as to: accuracy, storage in a secure way and access arrangements for especially sensitive information etc. For example, these records would include attendance registers for practitioners and children, administration of medication to children, visitors to the provision, risk and health and safety audit records.

- Monitoring the conduct and behaviour of adults within the provision, including child care practitioners and support staff within the team, professional visitors, parents and

Act as a role model

The nurturing care of children is focused on their emotional wellbeing wider family members. For example, ensuring that 'heated discussion' or arguments, particularly sensitive or confidential conversation, or interaction generally unsuitable for children to witness, is conducted outside of their environment.

While this range of Registered Person responsibilities is not intended to be exhaustive, it does highlight the breadth of awareness required for the role. It also demonstrates the importance of the Registered Person being able to adopt a sufficiently objective overview of what is and is not happening within the provision, whether a home environment for a childminder, or manager within a group care provision. Based on daily observation and the piecing together of these, over time, it also highlights the significance of the Registered Person actively owning their authority and being able to practice with professional confidence. A more detailed examination of this Registered Person role is explored in Chapter 7.

Designated or Lead Person for Safeguarding

The EYFS Safeguarding and Welfare Requirements specify the need for a practitioner within the provision to hold the position of Designated or Lead Person for Safeguarding – referred to in this book as the Designated Person as this is the term referred to in a number of other professional guidance documents, including for schools, health provision and GP practices – it also gives an indication as to the importance attributed to this role.

Across most professional disciplines the Designated Person role is held by a manager or practitioner with considerable experience in work with children and families, including in the area of safeguarding. In schools for example, this role is often held by the head teacher or the manager of the school's family support or home/school liaison team. What is fundamental is that this person needs the requisite knowledge, skills, abilities and professional maturity to fulfill the role. As outlined in the previous section of this chapter, the Designated Person should hold a similar level of authority to the Registered Person and be competent in taking an objective and thorough overview of the complex web of relationships between children, their families, the key person, the full practitioner team and wider children's service, professional network. Although the Designated Person role includes some strategic elements, it is primarily an operational role focused on making the provision's safeguarding responsibilities easily understood by all parties in a practical way. This role will be examined in greater detail in Chapter 4.

LINKS WITH YOUR PRACTICE

Safeguarding connects to all aspects of practice. It means:

- Ensuring that the physical environment is safe and secure, that any risks or threats to the provision are minimised and that practitioners own their responsibility to support each other in modeling mature adult behaviour, as reflected in their provision's code of professional conduct

- Providing an emotionally warm and nurturing environment for children and parents alike, including a reliable pattern or routine to the day upon which children can rely and that prioritises the stimulation of their emotional and social development

- Adopting a comprehensive approach to the way that the EYFS Safeguarding and Welfare Requirements are integrated into day-to-day practice through a suite of clear policy and procedural guidance

- Being thoughtful in the application of policy and procedure, in order that a regimented response is avoided and the individual needs of the unique child are fully embraced

- Making sure that safeguarding specific policy reflects professional responses to children and parents' needs across the full safeguarding spectrum, including provision of clear child protection, whistle-blowing and allegations against practitioners procedures

- Emphasis to the importance of the Designated Person for Safeguarding role and attendant responsibilities are fully recognised within the provision, that the person holding this role is given ample opportunity to attend specialist training to enhance the provision's practice and holds sufficient authority to challenge others, as appropriate

- Managerial responsibility to model high standards of practice in safeguarding is reflected in the leadership of the provision, including in a thoroughly embedded approach towards the way that practitioners are recruited, inducted, deployed, trained, guided, managed and supervised.

Bringing it all together: 'Safer' attitudes, behaviour and relationships

A 'safe' organisation relies on all of the elements laid out in this chapter, to provide firm foundations. It is made fully effective, however, by the ways in which practitioners present and conduct themselves daily. The people are what make any organisation after all, not the beautifully bound and colourful procedures. It is the people, including the childminder or group care provider manager and the support and assistance of their respective teams, who actively put their philosophy, policies and procedures into practice and bring it all to life. This softer, but all important dimension includes each and every childcare practitioner being:

- Alert, interested and engaged in their work

- Willing to put themselves out and 'go the extra mile' in providing an individual and sensitive service to children and their families

- Physically, emotionally and psychologically well and fit for work

- Willing to reflect and challenge their own values, perceptions and ideals

- Responsive to colleagues' (or family members'), feedback, willing to receive others' observation in a mature, professional way (rather than as personal attack) and able to discuss a range of opinions in identifying a route forward

- Responsible to challenge the practice and conduct of their work colleagues and whistle-blow, if required

- Accountable for errors, misjudgements or mistakes in their work and willing to apologise, learn from the experience and move on

- Able to consider their professional development as an ongoing journey, willing to attend and participate in training courses and engage in making changes to their practice, in order to offer an enhanced service to children and their families

- Honest with themselves, including owning up to times during which their passion and enthusiasm for working with children and families has temporarily or permanently died, able to review their professional commitments and if necessary, take steps to move on.

The Early Years Foundation Stage 2012 specifies that written policies and procedures for home-based childcare provision is no longer a requirement. Whilst the intention of this National policy change is to reduce the demands on childminders to produce extensive paperwork, my belief is that high quality child care is represented in the form of clear written policy and procedural guidance. This serves to represent the childminder's philosophy, including what parents can expect both in the form of a professional partnership and shared care of their child.

Although there is no 'fail-safe' blueprint for safeguarding children, their families and practitioners, appraising your provision against the content of the last three chapters will go a long way towards establishing a reliable structure and culture against which to practise every day.

In the next five chapters we will continue with our journey by looking at safeguarding, including child protection, in a much more specific way.

*A full exploration of practitioners' safeguarding roles and responsibilities across this spectrum will be addressed in Chapter 4.

KEY POINTS IN CREATING AN EFFECTIVE INTERFACE BETWEEN POLICY AND PROCEDURE

- Safeguarding is central to absolutely everything that happens within a provision. The links should be obvious to all practitioners, whether, for example, this is in providing a warm, secure environment or there being a clear relationship between policy and daily practice

- Although the Registered Person and manager are responsible for setting up the foundations for high standards of practice, all practitioners need to be professionally competent, emotionally available to fulfill their role as a key person, vigilant and skilled in their performance

Chapter 4

The safeguarding task: Practical approaches

In this chapter we are going to get much more specific with regards to our safeguarding, including child protection, roles and responsibilities. We will look at the day-to-day practicalities, including:

- What the term 'safeguarding' means

- What the provision should have in place regarding safeguarding responsibilities

- Working with children and their families across the full safeguarding spectrum

- A practical model for 'balancing' risk, harm and need along aside strengths and protective factors

- Identifying 'clues' to secure and insecure attachment patterns

- The role of the Designated Person for Safeguarding.

What safeguarding means

The term 'safeguarding' refers to practitioner's duties to:

- Protect children

- Prevent impairment to their growth and development

- Promote their well-being.

As babies and small children are entirely dependent on adults to have their needs met, practitioners are responsible for ensuring that they work in meaningful partnership with parents or any other key attachment figures in the child's life.

Effective safeguarding includes taking explicit ownership of your responsibilities, in partnership with parents

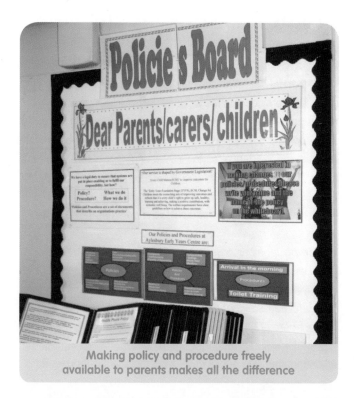

Making policy and procedure freely available to parents makes all the difference

As discussed in Chapters 1-3, practitioners' safeguarding responsibilities are strongly focused on offering early help to children and their parents. This includes helping to identify low-level needs for either children or their parents at the earliest opportunity, providing help and support ourselves and/ or getting children and parents linked-up to other professional services and therefore helping to prevent needs becoming impairments or harm.

At the most serious end of safeguarding concerns, sits child protection. This includes situations in which practitioners' concerns for children have become so great that they believe the child is being significantly harmed or their health or development is being significantly impaired. Let's consider a live example here.

This case study (opposite) demonstrates well the range of responsibilities that fall within the safeguarding remit for all child care practitioners. Central to this, as outlined in Chapters 1-3, is that we have built honest, open relationships between ourselves as professional practitioners and children and their families. This provides the firm foundation upon which ethical safeguarding practice is based. We will now move on to consider how legislation, guidance and early years sector professional standards guide our roles and responsibilities in safeguarding and child protection.

Meeting the specific safeguarding requirements of the EYFS

The Childcare Act 2006 lays out the legal framework for early years providers in the way that they provide childcare. With regard to safeguarding, the specific responsibilities are detailed in the EYFS Safeguarding and Welfare Requirements. The statutory guidance to the EYFS also makes clear that all provisions are expected to work to:

- *What to do if You're Worried a Child is being Abused* (2006)

- *Working Together to Safeguard Children* (2010, currently under review)

- *Information Sharing: Guidance for practitioners and managers* (2008).

Taken together, this guidance lays out the specific requirements

for each provision to respond in a comprehensive way to their safeguarding responsibilities.

This includes the requirement for each provision to have a safeguarding policy that links all aspects of day-to-day practice to the professional role of safeguarding; it should also point the reader in the direction of accompanying procedures to detail the action to be taken in particular situations.

The safeguarding policy should include the following:

- Reference to the fact that the provision **follows the law** in providing a truly professional standard of care to children and their families

- Arrangements for sharing information with parents (or those with parental responsibility), about safeguarding children procedures, before the child joins the provision and at regular intervals throughout their attendance

- Explicit reference to the relationship between sharing information and managing confidentiality, including examples of what parents can expect from practitioners

- Roles and responsibilities of individual practitioners and managers in safeguarding and promoting the welfare of children, including identifying 'clues' to harm or need in the child or parent, recording these observations and sharing this information both with parents and other professionals

- The way in which parents will be involved in the child protection process, including the very few circumstances in which it is not appropriate for them to be informed that a referral to Children's Social Care is about to be made. For example, in situations where the parent poses an immediate risk to themselves and/or the child, has threatened extreme violence and is in denial, or suffering significantly poor mental health or where sexual abuse to the child is suspected

- The name of the provision's Designated Person for safeguarding, their role and responsibilities and how they can be contacted

- The steps to be taken when a concern about a child's or parent's welfare, or safety and/or well-being is raised, including how this will be recorded

Example: Objective overview

A meaningful, day-to-day relationship with parents as partners, makes asking sensitive questions much easier

Jamelia is three-years-old and the middle child of three. She has an older brother of seven years and a younger brother of nine months. Jamelia started coming to the setting just over six months ago. During the last two months, though, it has become noticeable that her social and emotional development have slowed down. Practitioners have heard her using very little language, where just a few months ago she was making clear sentences. She has also reverted to playing alone or along aside other children whereas before she had begun to play more co-operatively with others. She seems to have lost a great deal of weight too.

Out of the blue, the nursery manager received a call from a health visitor making enquiries about Jamelia and her family. She asked whether Jamelia was attending the nursery and if the manager knew why Jamelia had failed to attend the last two appointments at the Coeliac Clinic. As the nursery manager and health visitor talk with each other, it becomes clear that Jamelia's mum has omitted to inform the nursery of Jamelia's specific health needs. It also comes to light that Jamelia had a younger sister who died in unusual circumstances, eighteen months ago. The baby

had been six-weeks-old. Her death had been recorded as unexplained by the coroner. The health visitor tells the nursery manager that she believes that the baby was found dead by the children.

I imagine, like me, you have a great number of questions you would like to ask Jamelia's mum. It is also important to remember that the way in which we ask these questions will set the tone for how we continue to work together into the future. We need to make sure to 'keep ourselves in check' including:

- Not to jump to conclusions or enter into making value judgements about Jamelia's mum

- Not to overreact on an emotional level and enter into discussion while being driven by emotions

- Not to assume that, because the health visitor is a fellow professional, what she told the manager is factually accurate (keep in mind that professionals can dramatise and/or minimise accounts of family life).

Example: Objective overview

I am confident that you would want to check what the health visitor has said and compare this to your own observations on the changes in Jamelia's well-being and development. This information can then be placed in the context of both our prior relationship with Jamelia's mum, as well as what she might say when we talk with her about the telephone call from the health visitor.

A sensitive but focused discussion with Jamelia's mum should lead you to be able to make an assessment as to what should happen next.

For example, Jamelia's mum's willingness to have the conversation with you and her reactions during the discussion would tell you a great deal.

In the course of discussion, you should be able to make a baseline assessment of her emotional and mental health (i.e. is she deeply depressed or in denial about her baby's death?) and also gain insight into her understanding of her daughter's needs and how she is responding to them.

Sensitive but focused discussion

Only through entering into a sensitive, detailed and focused conversation with Jamelia's mum would it be possible to make an initial judgement as to whether:

- Her emotional and/or mental health is impacting on her capacity to parent the children

- She understands her daughter's health care needs

- She intentionally withheld information from the nursery on Jamelia's health needs

- She actively chose to discontinue attendance at the Coeliac Clinic

- She is providing any treatment for her daughter's coeliac disease

- She cares for Jamelia differently, compared to her sons

- She recognises the significance of bereavement on her own and/or the children's well-being

- She has insight into her current parenting capacity, how she might have parented in the past and what might be expected of a responsible parent.

Your initial assessment of the interaction with Jamelia's mum should give you a clear idea as to whether it appears that she is (intentionally or unintentionally) impairing, further impairing and/or significantly impairing her child (Children Act 1989, Section 17) and/or significantly harming her child (Children Act 1989, Section 31).

Whatever your initial assessment tells you, you have a legal responsibility to ensure that Jamelia's needs are responded to appropriately and her mum is supported in acting as a responsible parent.

The practitioner who holds the Key Person role for Jamelia would be the person most suited to enter into discussion with Jamelia's mum. They might do this in partnership with the manager who received the call from the health visitor. The designated person for safeguarding might also maintain an objective overview to ensure that Jamelia's needs are maintained as a central focus.

The Designated Person for Safeguarding needs to be easily identified by parents and practitioners alike

A safe environment should be maintained for children

- The procedure for referring concerns about a child's and/or parent's welfare, safety or well-being to local statutory children's services (or vulnerable adults' agencies), including children's social care and/or the police child abuse investigation team

- The professional code of conduct for the provision, (including for the childminding household), which indicates the expected standards of child care practice and specific guidance on how practitioners do and do not behave in their professional capacity

- How to make an allegation or complaint against a practitioner and/or setting – who to contact and what to expect

- The procedure to be followed in the event of an allegation being made against a practitioner, member of the childminding household, student, trainee or volunteer by a child, parent, member of the public or professional from another discipline or provision

- How practitioners' knowledge of safeguarding children and their families is kept up-to-date and the focus for ongoing skills development for practitioners within the provision.

The Designated Person for Safeguarding within the provision, in consultation with the Registered Person and manager (roles which may be held by the same or different people), is responsible for co-ordinating all aspects of safeguarding practice.

The role of the Designated Person for Safeguarding

As indicated in Chapter 3, it is essential that the Designated Person for Safeguarding is able to adopt an objective overview for the entire provision and has sufficient capacity to assess and analyse what they observe. As they are accountable for holding both a general and specific vision for the provision with regard to safeguarding, they need to possess the professional **competence** and **confidence** for ensuring that this vision becomes a reality, in practical day-to-day terms. For this reason the Designated Person must hold sufficient authority to influence unit planning and management at both an operational and strategic level. Although the Designated Person need not necessarily hold a managerial role, it is vital that they are held in high regard by the team and are able to challenge managers in a positive way to effect change, as appropriate.

Childminders engaged in home-based care of children naturally hold both the Registered Person and designated person role and responsibilities. In a similar way to designated persons within group care provision, they must assume authority and accountability for their family unit at all times, i.e. both during the hours that professional child care is provided and outside these hours.

In order to ensure that the Designated Person holds the requisite knowledge, skills, abilities, attitudes and professional maturity to fulfill this role, it is essential that they receive regular training and opportunities for professional development.

On a day-to-day basis the Designated Person has a responsibility to ensure that:

- Every practitioner (including cook, premises officer, students etc.) is aware of their individual legal responsibility to safeguard and protect children within the provision

- All practitioners are familiar with the provision safeguarding policy, including the child protection procedures and are aware that their role is to **observe**, **record** and **report** their concerns for a child, parent, wider family member or practitioner to the designated person

- Support and advice are provided in such a way that seeks to develop and promote practitioners' professional confidence

- Practitioners are supported in fulfilling their safeguarding, including child protection, responsibilities. This might involve 'on the floor' supervision, as well as a more intensive level of guidance and support during times that child protection processes are proving more personally demanding to practitioners

- Either they (as the Designated Person) co-ordinate contact with the wider Children's Service professionals, including Children's Social Care when making a formal child protection referral, or closely support practitioners in making these contacts

- All written records of observations, dialogue with parents and information gathered within the provision distinguishes between what is factual information and what is professional opinion based on observation, assessment and analysis

- Written records are legible, dated, signed and maintained to a high professional standard and kept confidentially

- They act as a key point of contact, as the named Designated Person for the provision, in relation for a range of outside professional agencies

- High standards of professional interaction with the wider Children's Services are established and maintained, in such

a way that effective inter-professional collaboration as an integrated 'team around the child' is made a reality

- Professional practitioners within the wider Children's Services are appropriately challenged at times when ill-judged, inadequate or misinformed responses are received. This includes the designated person's responsibility to escalate challenge through the Children's Services management hierarchy as necessary and appropriate

- A safe environment is maintained for children, their families and the practitioner team in the ways identified in Chapters 1-3

- Professional practice within the provision is maintained to a high standard. This includes monitoring and identifying 'blurred boundaries' between practitioners in their relationships with children and parents and intervening in such a way to enable good standards to be restored. On occasion it might also be necessary to employ the whistle blowing, disciplinary and/or allegations against practitioners procedures, as appropriate.

The role of the Designated Person is professionally demanding and requires a dynamic, reflective and pro-active practitioner, who is committed to developing the practitioner team. The Designated Person role will be explored in greater depth in Chapter 7.

Working with children and their families across the full safeguarding spectrum

As identified in the preceding chapters, practitioners' safeguarding responsibilities apply to all children and their families on a universal level of service provision. This means that all practitioners would naturally talk with parents about their safeguarding role from the outset of their relationship and at regular junctures as particular safeguarding matters arise, in the media for example, and on occasions when specific safeguarding concerns arise for the child and/or their parent.

At the initial stage of relationship-building with a new child and parent, it would be appropriate to outline the policies and procedures to which all childcare practitioners work. This should be done incrementally, over time, rather than bombarding parents with huge amounts of information at the early stage of relationship-forming. It might be supported by giving the parent a copy of the safeguarding policy and perhaps even a copy of the *What to Do if You're Worried a Child is Being Abused* (2006) summary guidance. This should be supported by an explanation of how it all translates to daily practice. To make my point about the importance of the conversations we have with parents, let me draw on a similar example from my own day-to-day, domestic life. Have you read the instruction manual for your washing machine? I have not. I listened politely as the service engineer installed the washing machine and even asked some questions, but I did not look at the manual until something went wrong.

I suggest that this is the same for most parents; they are interested in your safeguarding responsibilities, but in their opinion it is never likely to apply to them, so they do not see the need to worry about the exact detail. That is, until they do. This is the stage when they might reach for the policy in the kitchen drawer, perhaps say that they had no idea that you held this safeguarding role, or what it might mean to them or their child. This is why it is important to talk honestly with parents about your range of safeguarding, including child protection responsibilities. It both keeps them well-informed and holds the channels of communication open, should they want to raise any concerns with you.

Before continuing with what responding to children and families across the full safeguarding spectrum means to day-to-day practice, on the page overleaf are some great examples of professional practice at this universal level, shared on a recent three-part safeguarding module.

Working with children and their families across the entire safeguarding spectrum, means much more than just focusing on your child protection responsibilities. We are going to explore what it means, using a live case study to help illustrate. There is also a diagram on page 41 that can aid in understanding this.

As demonstrated at the beginning of this section, practitioners hold safeguarding responsibilities at a *universal level*. This, as I have mentioned, will involve talking with parents on a regular basis about what they can do to safeguard and protect their children. It might include:

● Having an ongoing dialogue that focuses on the child's development, health and well-being

● Helping parents to develop an approach when vetting a babysitter or toddler gym club or an entertainer for their son's birthday party

● Discussing the importance of monitoring what children watch on television and installing child locks on the computer to bar access to unsuitable internet sites

Involve parents in development and review of policy, as National safeguarding matters arise.

Give the parent a copy of the safeguarding policy

Example: Talking with parents openly

Words often did not exist in the preferred language

Cedars is a small crèche that runs within a community college. Children attend the crèche on both a one-off or regular basis dependent on the kind of education or classes their parent is accessing. Before attending safeguarding training, three of the practitioners said that they had handed out parent's copies of their safeguarding policy, for them to read in their own time. When attending further training however, they shared that they had developed a wall display on safeguarding, made up of mostly visual images and as their crèche attracted parents of differing ethnicity, nationality, religion and language, they had supported their visual display with individual conversations with parents. One of the practitioners talked about this being very enlightening, as she discovered that subtle differences in understanding became clear when conversation was conducted in English. When her colleague talked with the parent in her preferred home language, however, a much greater level of mutual understanding became possible. As some of these practitioners represent the rich diversity from which a number of parents come, much greater detailed communication could be entered into. The practitioner stressed their professional learning and outcomes from this 'project' were as follows:

a) Words often did not exist in the preferred language for some concepts that needed to be explored. New language was therefore introduced in English, with detailed explanation in the preferred language, to help make the concepts fully understood

b) During the course of discussion, a mother asked quite detailed questions about abusive relationships between adults. As her enquiries became more specific, the practitioner suspected this woman was subject to domestic abuse in her marriage and felt it appropriate to ask her a direct question. As a result of this exchange, the practitioner has both referred the woman to a local service for women experiencing domestic abuse and recorded her disclosure on her child's record

c) Parents being appreciative of the practitioners' desire to make sense of what safeguarding means, particularly in the context of UK law. As a follow-up, the team planned a session on cultural practices in childrearing, some of which are against the law. These included female genital mutilation, spirit possession and exorcism and use of cultural herbal remedy (from which a child in the local authority was poisoned and died).

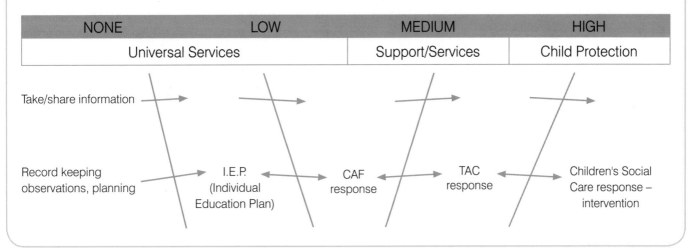

Safeguarding spectrum diagram of intervention

Level of concen/need/harm

NONE	LOW	MEDIUM	HIGH
Universal Services		Support/Services	Child Protection

Take/share information

Record keeping
observations, planning

I.E.P.
(Individual
Education Plan)

CAF
response

TAC
response

Children's Social
Care response –
intervention

- Assisting parents in developing ways to encourage their children to make confident choices and expanding ways that their children can safeguard themselves.

Practitioners have responsibilities at an **early intervention level**. This is where we have noticed that something is not quite right and, with a little support and assistance, matters can be prevented from turning into a much bigger difficulty. Providing 'early help' as Professor Eileen Munro (2011) refers to it, is in my opinion something that early years practitioners have a talent for.

For example, Baby Rommell arrived with June, his childminder, when he was seven-months-old. His mum, Charlene, was a psychiatric nurse and his dad, Dean, was an IT engineer who ran his own business from home. Rommell was the couple's first baby. June (the childminder), noticed early on that Charlene and Dean provided a high level of basic, physical care for Rommell's needs, but that Charlene was a little mechanical in handling her son. June noticed that Charlene talked with Rommell very little, handed him to June a bit like a parcel and that Rommell seemed a little more unsettled and watchful of his mum. With Dean, on the other hand, June noticed that Rommell seemed more relaxed and that she would often hear the loud babbling between them, coming down the path in the morning, before Dean knocked on the door. June often saw Dean blowing raspberries on Rommell's cheeks or neck to which Rommell giggled and Rommell holding his arms up to Dean in the confident knowledge that Dean would pick him up.

As a highly experienced childminder, particularly in the care of babies, June talked with Charlene and Dean with great sensitivity and tact. She gently talked with Charlene about play activities for babies at Rommell's stage of development. June also gave a great deal of positive feedback to both Rommell's parents and made a particular point of commending Charlene on how very beautifully Rommell was cared for. Having set down some firm foundations for their relationship-building stage, June did not wait too long before she started to talk gently with Charlene about how difficult it can be to adapt to being a parent for the first time and how the media presents a rosy image of parenthood, while the reality can be very different. This kind of 'hanging' statement is often what will encourage a parent like Charlene to begin to talk more freely. For June, a very competent childminder, this, of course, was her intention.

Naturally this kind of early intervention by June with Charlene and Rommell would be aimed at encouraging a deeper level of attachment between Charlene and her son. This includes June gently 'nudging along' her relationship with Charlene and helping to develop greater confidence in Charlene as a parent who has a very special relationship to Rommell. All practitioners, like June, would not seek to exclude Dean from this early intervention work, but to help unite both the parents and themselves, in their common interest – Rommell's well-being, health and development. This, I am sure you can see, is very much June's professional role, to help promote the very early stages of Rommell's social and emotional development. What if Charlene does not respond though, or feels that June might be criticising her parenting?

At the more **targeted intervention level** it is common to initiate a more formal level of discussion with parents and to begin talking about working closely in partnership with other professional services. This is the early stages of the 'team around the child' and family approach. This approach is emphasised very strongly by Professor Eileen Munro (2011), Graham Allen (2011), Dame Clare Tickell (2011) and Right Honorable Frank Field (2010) as the most important stage, the stage during which the smallest interventions (or levels of help), can make the biggest difference.

At this stage, June asked to meet Charlene and Dean together, after the other minded children and parents had left. She explained that it was very usual to review how parents were feeling that their relationship with their childminder was progressing and stressed that of course they were all concerned about how well Rommell was doing. June talked a little about all of her experience in working with new parents and their babies; she then respectfully and with great sensitivity talked about her observations of how Rommell reacted to his mum and his dad. She emphasised all the strengths she saw and then gently introduced the 'sly' way that post-natal depression can sometimes creep up on mums. Dean, June noticed, leaned forward on the sofa and looked her clearly in the eyes and Charlene sat back a little. She looked upset. Neither Charlene nor Dean said anything. June talked quietly about her experience in helping mums to get help through this time and then suggested that, as a psychiatric nurse, perhaps Charlene might have had some of these thoughts herself. Charlene started to cry a little and said how useless she felt, saying "I can't even do this right".

With the 'spell' of post-natal depression broken, Dean asked some questions, both of Charlene and June, and they began to work out a plan for the way forward. June asked Charlene to use her experience in working with post-natally depressed mums herself (thus building on her strengths) and they looked at Charlene booking an appointment to see her GP and/or health visitor. June offered to look after Rommell in the waiting room or even to go to the appointment with Charlene if she wished. During this time June also kept reinforcing that, as Charlene knew, post-natal depression can cast a shadow over the joys of early parenting and that she had a right to enjoy being a mum. She also stressed that Rommell was a bright baby and he too showed his concern for his mum, in his own way. Together Charlene, Dean and June put together their plan, with both Charlene's and Rommell's needs placed very much as central focus. Naturally this very open and sensitive approach also empowered and supported Dean and gave him a clear message that he could talk with June at any time he chose.

What if Charlene and Dean had not reacted in this way though, or had taken exception to June 'interfering'?

At the more **formal targeted intervention level**, concerns for both the child and the parent become more serious and concerning. This is often when practitioners begin to see that a child is being harmed at a lower level and/or their health and/or development might be affected. This is the stage that requires a much more co-ordinated approach and formally involves work with professional practitioners from the wider Children's Services. It is also the point when the needs of the child and their parents are viewed as complex and the co-ordinated approach will often involve a Common Assessment Framework (CAF) to ensure that both the parents and professional practitioners are working together in an agreed way, as a 'team around the child' and family. This is a point when it would be appropriate for the Designated Person within the provision to contact Children's Social Care, to agree an appropriate way forward and to establish whether services are involved with the family already. It may, for example, be that the police have been called out to the address a number of times and that Children's Social Care has visited the family at home. It is important to remember, however, that this might not necessarily be known to the child care provision.

Returning to Rommell, Charlene and Dean and their work with June, let's imagine that things have become rather more concerning and there is a need for a much more co-ordinated response with other professional services.

Over a period of just three weeks, following June's formal meeting with Charlene and Dean, June has:

- Arrived to meet Charlene at the GP practice twice. Charlene arrived too late for the appointment though and still has not seen her GP

- Been told by Dean that Charlene has been drinking a great deal. He had said that on the days that he worked late, he got home at 7.30pm, to find Charlene fast asleep on the sofa and Rommell crying

- Noticed that Rommell's physical care has declined, he has often arrived in a very dirty nappy, has quite severe nappy rash and seems very hungry

- Noticed that Rommell's development seems to be regressing. He has not been communicating at all, smiles very little and is very difficult to settle

- Been told by Charlene that Dean has told her that she's a crap mum and that if she does not pull herself together he is leaving her.

In response to these developments, June made a telephone call to Children's Social Care about all of her concerns for the family and was told that the police have contacted Children's Social Care to inform them about domestic disputes at the address. Children's Social Care have agreed that June should begin a CAF with the family and approach the Family Support Team at the local Children's Centre and Rommell's health visitor to offer support. June also called her Childminding Network Co-ordinator to ask for help in starting a CAF, as she had never done this before.

Within just a few days June talked with both Charlene and Dean about the growing concerns she had for both of them and for Rommell. She invited them to come to meet her, which they agreed to do separately. She had also arranged a 'team around the child' meeting in 10 days time. When June met both Charlene and Dean they both reluctantly agreed that things had got out of control and that Rommell was not being looked after in the way he should be. Dean was a little more willing to come to the 'team around the child' meeting at June's house and told June that he might be moving out of the flat for a while, to allow things to cool down a bit between him and Charlene. He told June that he would probably go to his mum's and might take Rommell with him, if Charlene agreed. Charlene, on the other hand, was upset that June had taken things into her own hands, but agreed that she had not been looking after Rommell well enough. She said that she might not get to the meeting because of work commitments, but that she would try. (June had thought that Charlene was probably feeling under a great deal of pressure and was using work as an excuse to not engage in a meeting that she thought might be much too difficult to manage.)

As it happened, June's fears about Charlene were correct. Charlene did not attend the 'team around the child' meeting, but Dean, his mum, the health visitor and a family support worker did attend. Dean and his mum had already reached an agreement with Charlene that Rommell would continue to come to June every day, but he would stay with Dean and his grandma four nights per week. June and the other professionals were pleased that the family had already made some arrangements to take best care of Rommell, and saw this as a real strength. They agreed with Dean though, that Rommell's care and emotional/social development needed to

be closely monitored. It was also agreed that June would talk with Charlene about the plans from the meeting and ask her to meet with her health visitor and the family support worker, who said she could offer one-to-one help with Charlene, if she would agree to meet her. What if these plans with Dean and his mum and the agreement with Charlene for Rommell to stay at his grandma's home four nights per week, do not work out though?

At the **serious level of concern** – the level that is referred to as **child protection** – the concerns for practitioners are usually so great that they have either observed clear harm to the child or suspect harm will occur if they do not act. In these circumstances there might be great concern for the parent's capacity to parent their child and the parent may well be influenced by the effects of domestic abuse, drug or alcohol abuse, mental ill-health or physical/learning disability. In these situations the practitioner's responsibility is to contact Children's Social Care and to make a formal child protection referral. In most cases the practitioner would advise parents of their intention, including the reasons for making this call and remind the parents that as a professional child care practitioner, their primary, legal responsibility is to safeguard and protect the child. In a few situations however, it will not be appropriate to inform the parents that a call is to be made to Children's Social Care. These include all cases of suspected sexual abuse to the child and/or situations where the parent seems to pose an immediate risk to themselves and/or their child

Building a meaningful relationship with both parents is vital

i.e. they are 'out of control' with anger, are demonstrating the effects of severe mental health needs, at risk of acute physical threat etc. It should be remembered that Children's Social Care do not provide an emergency, blue light service. In the event of an emergency, the police and/or ambulance service should be called, as necessary and appropriate.

Returning to June's professional relationship with Charlene, Dean and his mum in the care of baby Rommell, let's take our concerns to a level that would represent the need for a child protection level of intervention. Let's imagine that initially the arrangement between Dean and his mum having Rommell for four evenings per week had been successful, but then communication between Charlene and Dean had broken down. Dean had informed June of this turn in events and was, with Charlene's agreement, popping around to see Rommell whilst he was at June's house. During a visit to June, Dean had expressed his concern for what he thought was an even greater deterioration in Charlene's mental health. During this conversation with Dean, June made it clear that she would continue to monitor Rommell's care closely, would record what Dean had told her and would exercise her child protection responsibility if she needed to.

Then, a few mornings later, Charlene had arrived with Rommell, in an unusually disheveled state, in unironed clothes, smelling of body odour and slightly unsteady on her feet. June had registered this significant change in Charlene's self-care and had attempted to encourage her to stay a little while, whilst she monitored Charlene's general well-being. As she was chatting with Charlene, she noticed that Rommell had a bloodshot eye and seemed listless and sleepy in her arms. Also that Charlene's speech was slurred, she looked as if she had been crying and she swung around to hurl abuse at an invisible person behind her. June noticed, as she leant forward to talk with Charlene, that she seemed very agitated and that engaging her in further conversation was not the thing to do. As June got up, saying to Charlene that she was going to get a bottle for Rommell, Charlene jumped up and said she needed to leave for work, otherwise she'd be late. As Charlene left, Rommell was violently sick. June's razor-sharp reaction led her to call for an ambulance, as she was concerned that Rommell was showing signs of concussion, including possible signs of having been shaken.

As June cleaned up the vomit and waited for the ambulance, she called Dean and asked him to meet her at the hospital. Once at the hospital and in the process of informing the house doctor of her concerns at Accident and Emergency, Dean arrived and June introduced him to the house doctor. Once Rommell's needs were being properly assessed, June excused herself and called Charlene to find out where she was. As June was still concerned for her well-being, she decided not to inform her that Rommell was at hospital, but to call Children's Social Care, to make a formal child protection referral. During this call, she outlined all of her initial concerns, advised Children's Social Care that Rommell was currently with his dad at the hospital and informed the duty officer of her concerns for Charlene's mental health.

Although very few child protection levels of concern will reach this level of complexity, I am sure you can see that June fulfilled her child protection responsibilities in a thorough way, always ensuring that she kept her primary focus upon Rommell and his needs. June demonstrates through her actions, at each level of intervention with Charlene and Dean, that her main concern was always for Rommell and she did everything within her remit to support and assist them in meeting their son's needs. This case study also, in my opinion, shows the vital importance of practitioners being well-informed about their safeguarding responsibilities across the entire safeguarding spectrum of intervention and indicates how important it is for practitioners to be knowledgeable, competent and confident in fulfilling their duties.

I also believe that this case study demonstrates that building professional relationships with parents – where they feel sufficiently confident to invest their trust – is essential. Without setting these firm foundations for working together at the relationship-building stage, Charlene and Dean would not have trusted June in the way they did. This includes the stage when Dean talked to June about his concern for Charlene's deteriorating mental health right up until the child protection stage, where Rommell had clearly been harmed and Charlene was in great distress. Charlene might have chosen to not bring Rommell to June on that day, but I suggest she did choose to bring him, whether this choice was on a fully conscious level or not, because she trusted that June would do the right thing.

A practical model for assessing safeguarding concerns

I am sure you have noticed the amount of times I referred to strengths while illustrating the different stages of intervention with Rommell, Charlene and Dean. This was intentional. The Assessment Framework guidance (2000) reminds us of the importance of identifying and actively working with strengths and protective factors when entering into any assessment with a child and their family. This assists us in taking a more balanced view; it also instills confidence with parents that we are seeing 'the good' as well as the 'not so good'. (This is exactly the kind of model we use when approaching behaviour management with children, i.e. we build on what is working.) In the same way, when engaging with parents to change what is not working with regard to their parenting of their child, impairment to their child's health and/or development and/or any harm, we need to start from what is working and then build from here, i.e, focusing on strengths and protective factors helps parents to see that change is achievable, as they have often been successful in aspects of their parenting before.

When entering into an assessment then, we would use the 'Assessment Framework triangle', which I feel sure you will be familiar with from attendance on safeguarding – including child protection – training. You should focus on the inter-relating

dimensions from each side of the triangle, concentrating on what your own observations and interactions with the child and their parents tell you. If you do not have one to hand, there is an example below.

You might also wish to refer to the categories of harm, from the *What to do if you're worried a child is being abused guidance* (2006). This will help to remind you of the kind of events, relationships and/or 'clues' that might suggest that a child might be, or, is being significantly impaired and/or harmed. A copy of the categories of abuse can be found at the end of this chapter.

I should also like to introduce you to this 'scales model' (shown on the page overleaf). I have introduced it to many local authorities, individual provisions and practitioners, who now use it in the course of their safeguarding work. It helps to keep

Assessment Framework: Framework for the assessment of children in need and their families (2000)

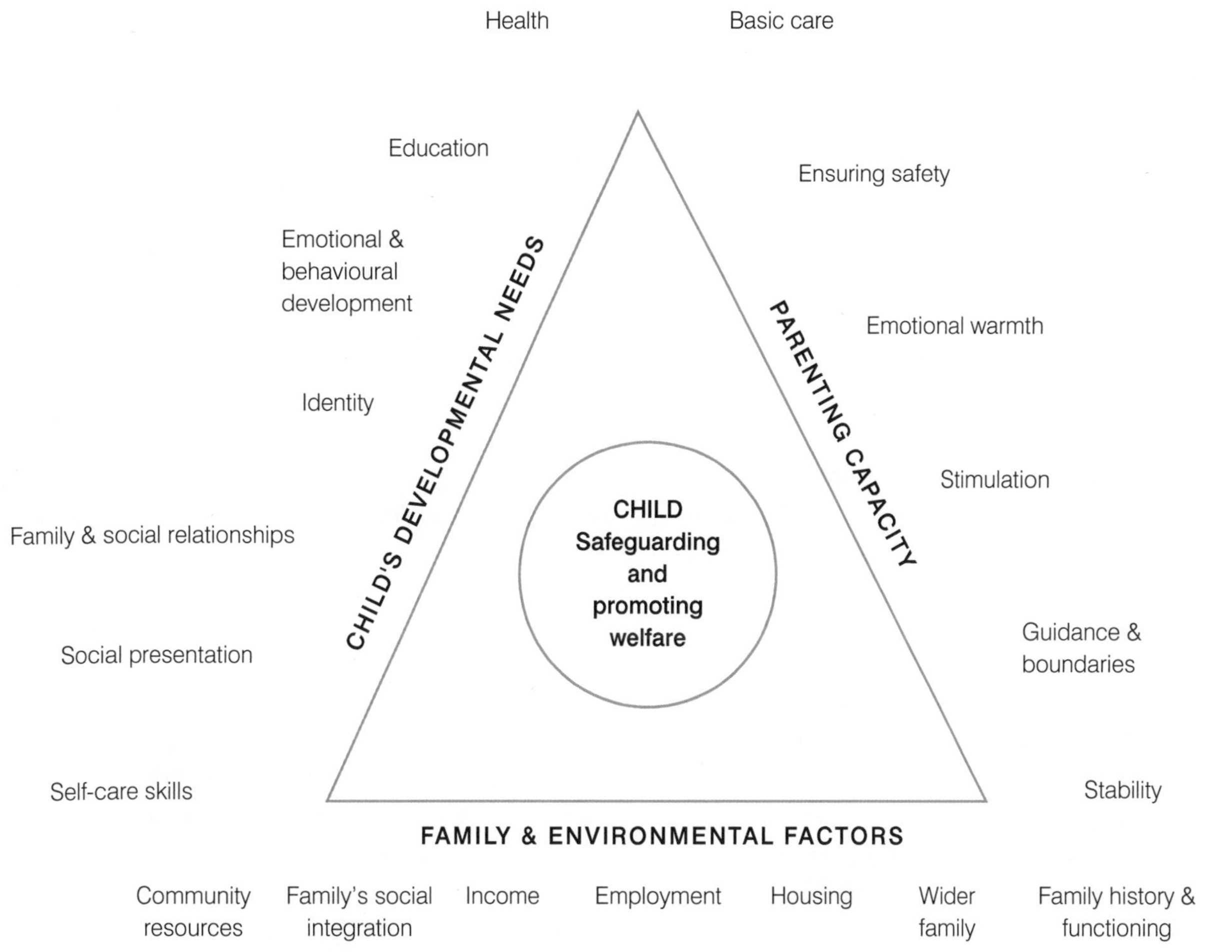

Health   Basic care

Education

Ensuring safety

Emotional & behavioural development

CHILD'S DEVELOPMENTAL NEEDS   PARENTING CAPACITY

Emotional warmth

Identity

Stimulation

CHILD Safeguarding and promoting welfare

Family & social relationships

Guidance & boundaries

Social presentation

Self-care skills

Stability

FAMILY & ENVIRONMENTAL FACTORS

Community resources   Family's social integration   Income   Employment   Housing   Wider family   Family history & functioning

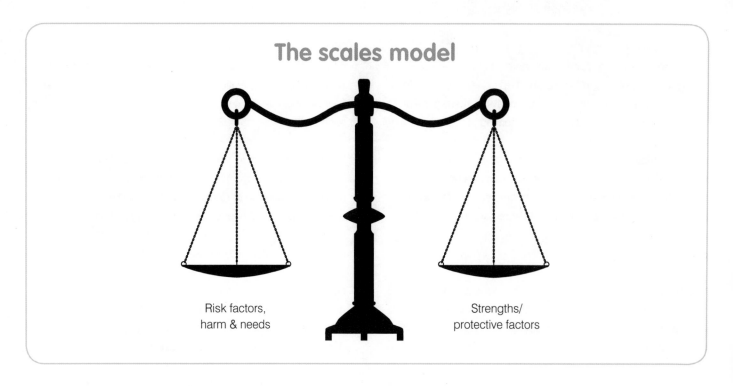

The scales model

Risk factors, harm & needs

Strengths/ protective factors

Balancing the risks against the strengths

Risk factors, harm and needs	Strengths/protective factors
Rommell's insecure attachment to Charlene	Charlene is bright and has professional insight into mental health needs
Reported level of Charlene's alcohol use (needs to be confirmed)	Rommell's secure attachment with Dean
Suspected post-natal depression in Charlene	Grandma seems happy to provide support to Charlene and Dean
Deterioration in the couple's relationship and Dean leaving the family home	Charlene and Dean are talking with each other and with June
Deterioration in Rommell's social/emotional well-being	Both Charlene and Dean agree with June, that their care of Rommell is not 'good enough'

a consistent approach in place, where risk, harm and need are balanced in relation to strengths and protective factors in their safeguarding work with children and their families. Rather than going into a lengthy explanation about how to use it, I am going to note the risks, harm and need and strengths/protective factors for Rommell, Charlene and Dean. I will enter the first five; I then suggest you consider the next five. You will probably get at least an even number of risks to strengths.

Balancing risks, harm and need in relation to strengths and protective factors in this way also helps you see where the greatest imbalance exists (see above). This will generally assist you in deciding where to start your work with the parents and consider whether you should be doing this work alone or with your professional partners from the broader Children's Service. Whatever your decision, this process is

best undertaken with the setting's Designated Person for Safeguarding. For practitioners who work alone, like June in the case study example, a more objective overview and professional support and advice, might be offered through a consultation with Children's Social Care, or Childminding Network Co-ordinator.

Sharing your scales model with the parents will also help them to appreciate your professional concerns for their child, understand your approach better and see, often in simple terms, what needs to change. As this 'managing the change' process is something practitioners would do as a part of a wider 'team around the child' and family approach, with other professionals within the Children's Service network, (particularly at the child protection level of concern), we will look in this in much greater detail in Chapter 5.

Finally, as referenced in Chapter 1, we will focus briefly on attachment patterns, including what we might specifically see between children and their parents, in practical terms.

Identifying 'clues' to secure and insecure attachment patterns

As you, the early years practitioner, are involved in children's most formative years, and very often with a number of pregnant women and their partners, (at the even earlier stage of pre-birth, baby development), you are in a prime position to influence the very earliest stages of attachment, i.e. the relationship-forming stage between parents and their children or the 'falling in love' stage. This fundamental early attachment, as indicated in Chapter 1, sets the blueprint for the baby's brain development and subsequent brain capacity, for the rest of the child's life.

As a newborn baby experiences her world, her brain is forming and reinforcing trillions of connections – or synapses. So, for example, in the time that it takes for her to be fed, thousands of new synapses are produced. At the same time, thousands of existing synapses are being used and therefore reinforced. When we consider this we realise how aware this baby is

of everything that is going on around her, she is particularly sensitive when her instinctive needs are not met, including no response or a poor/inconsistent response to her cries. This means that for the baby trapped in the domestic warzone where her mum and dad shuttle between providing 'just enough' attention to her basic needs, then completely ignore her while they emotionally, physically and sexually tear each other apart, *is* being significantly harmed on each and every occasion. Unable to fight or run away (like animals would do), the baby girl is trapped in this toxic environment. In the fear, her brain is flooded with cortisol, bathing her brain in a substance that we now know impedes brain development and is killing off her brain function.

As practitioners we see, hear and feel the 'clues' to toxic relationships and experiences for children; often these can be noticed in the patterns of interaction between children, including babies and their parents. An insecure or inconsistent attachment pattern between the parent and child might be 'picked up' by noticing elements or combinations of the following:

● A parent who ignores the child's needs to such a degree that the child is silent in their cot or buggy. The child might smile or even laugh in an artificial way, but watch the parent very closely. The parent's display of affection for the child might be gushing and intended for an audience, but might show little consistency or substance. The child meanwhile might respond a little like a wooden brick.

Be able to spot 'clues' to secure and insecure attachment between children and their parents

These can be noticed in the patterns of interaction between children, including babies and their parents

The parent's ability to provide comfort for the child, tells us a great deal about the quality of the attachment

A child who has been loved, nurtured and cared for soon starts showing this towards others

- The emotional temperature shown towards the child by the parent might be very cool and highly critical. In response the child might try to please the parent, including trying to 'read their needs and be very helpful'. This parent might be quite 'fixed' and inflexible in their approach to life, including their relationship with their child. The parent might be insensitive towards the child's psychological or emotional needs and the child, in response, might be emotionless, or very emotionally contained or very good at looking after others.

- A parent might look towards the child to fulfill their emotional needs. This might include the need to keep the baby very close, perhaps over-indulging or over-feeding and wrapping in cotton wool. In response the child might be watchful and needy of the parent, dependent on them for everything. The relationship might be very 'special and exclusive' and hold great risks for the child when putting down relationships with others, for they are likely to be punished or rejected by the parent, for their betrayal.

- Unsettled, unsure relationship between parent and child, perhaps with a child who whines or cries frequently to gain attention. This might invite a 'mirror image' response from the parent, where they reinforce the child's behaviour by slapping and/or snapping at the child, or cuddle or give sweets on

an erratic basis. And so the pattern repeats, sometimes the feedback from the parent is pleasant and sometimes not, but for the child, 'at least it *is* attention'.

I am sure that some of these patterns will be familiar, you may also be aware that they often are accompanied by a number of other concerns. If you add these concerns together they may often weigh very heavy on the risk, harm and need side of the scales. This detail will help inform the risk assessment that the designated person for safeguarding will make and therefore indicate the actions to be taken. As discussed, the actions might include following procedure to initiate a 'team around the child' and family approach, along with other professional services, or making a child protection referral to Children's Social Care.

The importance of attachment between children and their parents is immense, and as 'artists in human relationships' – especially those relationships evolved in the early foundation years of children's lives – it is crucial that the ability to identify and intervene in poor or insecure patterns of attachment is recognised as absolutely fundamental to our role. I therefore highly recommend that you make this the subject of frequent discussion at your practitioner meetings. Suggestions for further reading can be found on the References page at the end of this book.

Finally, before we close this section, let's look at what we would be able to identify in a secure attachment pattern. Firstly, we would recognise that the parent sees it as their role to provide for their child, as a responsible parent. In this they would be emotionally warm, sensitive, responsive, interested, flexible, predictable and consistent in the care of their child. What we might see in terms of observed interaction between parent and child might include:

- The parent being able to interpret what their baby's cry means, i.e. hungry, wanting a nappy changed, frightened or in pain?

- The parent knowing what their child likes and perhaps their individual strengths

- A close and intimate 'special language' or words are shared between parent and child

- Both parent and child look forward to seeing each other and show signs of being pleased when reunited

- The baby or child easily 'tucks in' to the parent for a cuddle or hug, i.e. it is obvious to you that this level of intimacy is familiar

- There is a 'mirroring' between parent and child. The dad smiles and the baby copies, or as with the Rommell, Charlene and Dean case study, Dean blows a raspberry on Rommell's neck and Rommell laughs.

Let us keep firmly in mind that this is the kind of start to life that all children deserve to have, as a basic human right. It is therefore essential that wherever signals of unsure or insecure attachment are uncovered, swift and decisive attention from practitioners is attracted. They should indeed actively intend to present themselves as 'irresistible partners in change' as it is at this stage that the biggest and most significant difference can be made.

Categories and definitions of abuse

Abuse and neglect are forms of maltreatment of a child. Somebody may abuse or neglect a child by inflicting harm, or by failing to act to prevent harm. Children and young people may be abused in a family or in an institutional or community setting, by those known to them or, more rarely, by a stranger, for example via the Internet. They may be abused by an adult or adults, or another child or children.

LINKS WITH YOUR PRACTICE

Early years practitioners' legal responsibilities towards children and their families includes understanding:

- What 'safeguarding' actually means and what should be happening in practical terms at all four levels of the spectrum. (Clear links are made to earlier chapters of the book in which the fundamental foundation stones to effective safeguarding practice were laid.)

- The need for ongoing partnership, including open, honest communication with parents

- Appropriate levels of information-sharing, with parents and wider Children's Service professional network of practitioners, both at the 'team around the child'/ opportunity for targeted intervention level and as professional concerns reach the child protection threshold

- The 'scales model' presented in this chapter, (or a similar kind of model) to assist practitioners and Designated Persons in the practical consideration of risks, harm and need factors for the child, parent and wider family, in relation to strengths and protective factors. Whatever model is used, it should be clearly linked to the legal guidance, including the Assessment Framework

- The distinct roles of the Key Person and that of the Designated Person for Safeguarding, including their responsibility to recognise and act on 'signals' of insecure attachment between babies, young children and their parents

- Key responsibilities of the early years' practitioner to recognise concerns as they reach both the point where targeted intervention would be the obvious next step and where concerns have reached a child protection level. This includes the procedure in gathering a 'team around the child' and family (including beginning a CAF), consulting Children's Social Care and then making a formal referral

- The difference in the roles and responsibilities of the early year's practitioner, as opposed to those of other professional partners including health, Children's Social Care and the Police Child Abuse Investigation Team.

Emotional abuse

Emotional abuse is the persistent emotional maltreatment of a child such as to cause severe and persistent adverse effects on the child's emotional development. It may involve conveying to children that they are worthless or unloved, inadequate, or valued only insofar as they meet the needs of another person. It may include not giving the child opportunities to express their views, deliberately silencing them or 'making fun' of what they say or how they communicate. It may feature age or developmentally inappropriate expectations being imposed on children. These may include interactions that are beyond the child's developmental capability, as well as over-protection and limitation of exploration and learning, or preventing the child participating in normal social interaction. It may involve seeing or hearing the ill-treatment of another. It may involve serious bullying (including cyber-bullying), causing children frequently to feel frightened or in danger, or the exploitation or corruption of children. Some level of emotional abuse is involved in all types of maltreatment of a child, though it may occur alone.

Neglect

Neglect is the persistent failure to meet a child's basic physical and/or psychological needs, likely to result in the serious impairment of the child's health or development. Neglect may occur during pregnancy as a result of maternal substance abuse. Once a child is born, neglect may involve a parent or carer failing to:

- Provide adequate food, clothing and shelter (including exclusion from home or abandonment)

- Protect a child from physical and emotional harm or danger

- Ensure adequate supervision (including the use of inadequate care-givers)

- Ensure access to appropriate medical care and treatment

- May also include neglect of, or unresponsiveness to, a child's basic emotional needs.

Physical abuse

Physical abuse may involve hitting, shaking, throwing, poisoning, burning or scalding, drowning, suffocating or otherwise causing physical harm to a child. Physical harm may also be caused when a parent or carer fabricates the symptoms of, or deliberately induces, illness in a child.

Sexual abuse

Sexual abuse involves forcing or enticing a child or young person to take part in sexual activities, not necessarily involving a high level of violence, whether or not the child is aware of what is happening. The activities may involve physical contact, including assault by penetration (i.e. rape or oral sex) or non-penetrative acts such as masturbation, kissing, rubbing and touching outside clothing. They may also include non-contact activities, such as involving children in looking at, or in the production of, sexual images, watching sexual activities, encouraging children to behave in sexually inappropriate ways, or grooming a child in preparation for abuse (including via the Internet). Sexual abuse is not solely perpetrated by adult males. Women can also commit acts of sexual abuse, as can other children.

These legal definitions are taken from:

- *Working Together to Safeguard Children: A guide to inter-agency working to safeguard and promote the welfare of children* 2010 (Sections 1.32-1.36) – Currently under review.

KEY POINTS IN THE SAFEGUARDING TASK: PRACTICAL APPROACHES

- Safeguarding is far bigger than just child protection. A purposeful approach to safeguarding includes the recognition that sensitivity and an obvious partnership with both parents and professionals from the wider Children's Service, is essential

- Support and intervention can be offered in the form of 'early help' to the child and their family, as a 'team around the child', including use of a CAF, or, as a referral to Children's Social Care at the point that the child protection threshold for concern has been reached

- Attention should always be clearly focused on the child and practitioners should be well-informed and well-supported by their provision's Designated Person for Safeguarding

Chapter 5

Making integrated working a reality: Multi-agency collaboration

Effective work with children and their families across the entire safeguarding spectrum requires a serious commitment to working as a key member of the multi-professional team that makes up the 'team around the child' and, in the case of a child subject to a child protection plan, a member of the 'core group'. Indeed, many of the highest profile deaths to children in this country, including Maria Colwell way back in 1973 and Baby Peter Connolly in 2007, were in large part due to poor levels of:

- Information sharing between professionals and confusion about when parents should be included in information sharing and when they should not

- Understanding about the relationship between information sharing and confidentiality

- Meaningful engagement between the parents and professional practitioners across all services

- Inter-professional relationship, including competitive, jealous and undermining behaviours

- Individual and shared professional opinion on what needed to change in the family, the plans for how to go about it and how risk would be assessed and managed

- Leadership, supervision and management, across each of the professional services.

The focus in this chapter will therefore be on the importance of practitioners taking confident ownership of their professional role, as a part of the wider professional network. Within this, some of the traps that early years practitioners and their wider provision can fall into will be explored; particularly when they feel less confident in safeguarding matters than other professionals and therefore, on occasion, less likely to assert themselves.

A need to transform our professional DNA

Early years practitioners are entirely focused on the growth, development and well-being of children under five years. This is what many have professionally trained in, some to degree level.

The sector has some talented, highly experienced and knowledgeable practitioners, but on a number of occasions professional confidence is not developed to the same level. This limitation can undermine the overall competence of the practitioner. The Key Person for the child and the family attending early years provision should be able to:

- Hold key information and knowledge of the child

- Have an intimate understanding of the child's emotional well-being, specific likes and dislikes and personal characteristics

- Have developed a close and meaningful partnership with the child's parents

- Hold a portfolio of observations of the child, including their relationship to their parent/s, other children and practitioners etc.

Example: Honest, open and truthful communication

A strong culture of support and trust

The practitioners from Aylesbury Early Years Centre are a good example of a very competent team, led by an inspirational, straight-talking manager. They recognise their nursery philosophy as 'honest, open and truthful communication with everyone'.

Within the team, there is a strong culture of support and trust. They have built this over many years and attribute much of their professional confidence to giving each other regular feedback. At full practitioner meetings, for example, they discuss a piece of work with a family and give each other feedback on what they did well.

Equally, they do not hold back in making it known if something might have been done differently; the message is always delivered in a constructive way. They comment on practitioner conversations they overhear with children and their parents, interactions they witness and struggles they overcome. In fact they are relentless!

It really is their heartfelt philosophy and includes everyone – the cook, the kitchen assistant, the management team and all practitioners. In short, they have developed a capacity to be professionally reflective on a team level. There are some 'ways of talking' with each other that I have heard frequently within this team. These include the following brief examples:

- "I overheard you talking with Oyewo's mum this morning. She sounded angry about the fact that Oyewo had got paint on her clothes yesterday. I liked the way that you said that you understood that she was angry and then went on to explore how you could work together to prevent this happening again."

- "I know that you will forgive me if this is not true, but I have noticed that you seem a bit uneasy about talking with Sam's dad. Is that true? Is there anything that we can do in the team, to support you to building your relationship, as Sam's key worker?"

Although just a couple of brief examples, I am sure that you will be able to see the common threads in these 'ways of talking', i.e. they are designed to build on what is already working well (the key worker does talk to Sam's dad, rather than avoiding him), they are supportive of each other and intend to promote high standards of communication each and every day.

This knowledge is very individual, personal to the child and family and often includes detailed and specific nuances of human relationships. If the practitioner is unable to express this information with confidence to other professional members of the 'team around the child' or core group though, this vital information is lost, often with quite dramatic consequences. In the best case scenario the information might also have been communicated in writing and given an appropriate weight in the multi-professional assessment. However, in the worst situations, it might have been distorted, minimised or completely disregarded. The consequences can be dire, including the serious injury or death of a child.

If we are truly committed to being artists in human relationships, the early years sector needs to take itself in hand and concentrate on building professional confidence as a matter of urgency. Neglecting this responsibility could be seen as a safeguarding matter in itself – if we do nothing to transform our confidence as a professional body, we are inadvertently contributing to the risks faced by children. We are, after all, the adults here and if we truly care for children, we *will* make this professional journey. Practitioners need to be able to speak with power and authority, in a self-assured and confident way. This is vital if practitioners are to undertake their safeguarding role effectively.

If we are to truly and proudly own our profession, then we need to change the professional DNA to one that can be relied upon as:

- Confident

- Honest and principled

- Of high standard

- Well-informed and up to date

- Constantly questioning and reflective

- Professionally competent, in all senses.

We will expand upon the need for this urgent development in Chapters 7 and 8.

Information-sharing guidance

As outlined in the introduction to this chapter, the information-sharing guide to all professional practitioners involved in

Children's Services is probably one of the most misunderstood pieces of guidance.

Essentially the guidance philosophy is that information should be shared with parental knowledge and agreement. Gaining parental agreement can be easily managed and, as discussed in Chapter 2, is most effectively done within the context of the parent/Key Person relationship.

Some professional practitioners are still misinformed by the links between data protection and information sharing. The message is however quite clear in the guidance, as follows:

- The Data Protection Act 1998 does not prevent information sharing, but provides a guide to what is shared, by whom and for what purpose

- An open and honest approach with families sets you on a clear footing

- Agreement and consent should be sought from parents, unless doing so would be unsafe or inappropriate. (This might include cases where, for example, a child has been harmed, or, is at risk of harm and the parent is mentally unwell, such as the baby Rommell scenario in Chapter 4.)

- Information sharing should be 'measured' and proportionate when sharing without parental consent

- Practitioners should be mindful of sensitive information, including what might need to be treated as confidential (for example a parent's HIV status or previous marriage, might be completely irrelevant to agreeing a 'team around the child' approach to a child's additional needs and behaviour)

- Be accurate, provide information in a timely way and in a secure form

- Recorded in a detailed and clear way – i.e. what was shared, why and to whom?

- Advice should be sought if it is unclear whether information should be shared (*Information Sharing: Pocket Guide*, DCSF 2008 – Seven golden rules for information sharing).

If you and your provision are not familiar with this guidance, then it is advised you order or download it, especially with focus on the 'seven golden rules'.

We are going to return to take a more detailed look at Jamelia's case study from Chapter 4. The intention is to explore working with a broader array of professionals within the Children's Services, in a collaborative and meaningful way. As you re-read the case study (on the opposite page), notice the appropriate level of information that the health visitor shared with the nursery manager. We would agree that there are concerns for Jamelia as a 'child in need' as she does not seem to be receiving specialist medical support for coeliac disease.

Being the 'keepers' of current early years knowledge

In early years provision, our role is to **identify** concerns, **share** them, as appropriate within the wider Children's Service professional network and where the concerns are at a serious level, **refer** to Children's Social Care, as a child protection matter. As detailed throughout this book, this role includes keeping focus on:

- The child's individual and unique growth, development and well-being at different stages

- Detailed and frequent observations of the child

- The interaction between the child and their parent/s

- Any difference in the way this child is cared for within their family, as compared to their siblings.

It will be necessary to compare this child and their family to other similar children in order to demonstrate the difference. The Children Act 1989 (CA 1989), Section 31 (9) says "Where the question of whether harm has been suffered by a child is significant turns on the child's health or development, his health or development shall be compared to a similar child". This reference to 'comparing the child to a similar child' is very important to practitioners as we are 'the keepers of *what is* usual growth and development', across a particular developmental range.

Of the estimated 3,000 three-year-olds I have worked with, the vast majority have been growing and developing according to the expected range. Drawing on this professional knowledge and experience allows me to say, for example, that:

- Most 'reasonable parents' in Jamelia's mum's position would ensure that their daughter is receiving appropriate parenting and medical treatment to assist in promoting her health and development

- The fact that Jamelia's mum does not appear to be acting in this way suggests that she, as the parent, is playing a part in further impairing, significantly impairing and/or significantly harming her daughter.

Accurate daily records help to inform more detailed joint professional decision making, should this be necessary

Effective information sharing with parents happens successfully in the context of a warm relationship, with their focus clearly set on the child

Example: Working effectively as a 'team around the child'

Play a confident part in the 'team around the child' approach

Let's refresh our memory: Jamelia is three-years-old and the middle child of three. She has an older brother of seven years and a younger brother of nine months. Jamelia started coming to nursery just over six months ago. During the last two months though, it has become noticeable that her social and emotional development have slowed down. Practitioners have heard her using very little language, where just a few months ago she was making clear sentences. She has also reverted to playing alone or alongside other children, whereas before she had begun to play more co-operatively with others. She seems to have lost a great deal of weight too.

Out of the blue, the nursery manager received a call from a health visitor making enquiries about Jamelia and her family. She asked whether Jamelia was attending the nursery and if the manager knew why Jamelia had failed to attend the last two appointments at the Coeliac Clinic. As the nursery manager and health visitor talked with each other, it became clear that Jamelia's mum had omitted to inform the nursery of Jamelia's specific health needs. It also came to light that Jamelia had a younger sister who died in unusual circumstances, eighteen months ago. The baby

had been six-weeks-old. Her death had been recorded as unexplained by the Coroner. The health visitor told the nursery manager that she believes the baby was found dead by the children.

Our understanding of Jamelia and her family's needs might alter quite significantly, based on the information given to the nursery manager by the health visitor. However, I would expect that the manager will have questioned some of the information being provided by the health visitor, ensuring that:

● The health visitor did, in fact, know Jamelia and her family

● That the Jamelia who attends the nursery is, in fact, the same child that the health visitor is referring to and there is no error with regard to the child or family's identity

● The details regarding Jamelia's health needs and the death of a baby eighteen months earlier, are factually correct

● 'Softer' information with regard to Jamelia's mum's understanding of her daughter's health needs and

Example: Working effectively as a 'team around the child'

reactions to the death of a baby eighteen months earlier, are gathered.

Potential hazards in working together

It is important to treat this information with a healthy level of professional scepticism or reservation. I am not suggesting that the health visitor would lie to the nursery manager, but practitioners should be mindful of the ways in which information is communicated and how easily this can be distorted. This might include a sensationalist, dramatic approach or even one that minimises or refers to the highly emotional experiences of this family in a clinical and cool way. The potential for value judgements or stereotypes being attributed to families should not be under-estimated either. We should also remember that one of our key responsibilities, when working in partnership with a wider professional network of practitioners, is to challenge each other in the way in which we transmit key information.

I suggest you cover the text after the following questions and discuss this case study in a practitioner meeting. This will help to expand your capacity to hypothesise, or consider things from different perspectives. Ask yourselves:

- What concerns you?

- What possible explanations there might be for changes to Jamelia's well-being and development? (Consider many, rather than focusing on just one.)

- What possible explanations might there might be for Jamelia's mum apparently not providing the nursery with relevant details on Jamelia and the family history?

- How you would enter into conversation with Jamelia's mum (what might you actually say or ask?).

I hope that facilitated a really lively discussion in your team! You can uncover this next section now. This is not intended to be an exhaustive list, but I would suggest to find out:

- Whether Jamelia's mum knows the health visitor, and her description of the nature of their relationship

(for example, perhaps they fell out at about the time of the baby's death or they disagree about the treatment of Jamelia)

- Jamelia's mum's understanding of her daughter's health needs, including whether she accepts this diagnosis or description of coeliac disease or understands this in another way

- What Jamelia's mum does and does not do in responding to her daughter's health needs (she may be 'treating' Jamelia using other methods for example)

- Whether Jamelia did have a baby sister and if so, what happened to her (i.e. the circumstances of the baby's death)

- How Jamelia's mum has responded to her bereavement, both for herself and the children, including how she believes the children have understood the baby's death

- What explanation Jamelia's mum might have for the changes in Jamelia's emotional and social well-being (language and social interaction with other children)

- What explanation Jamelia's mum has for Jamelia's weight loss

- How Jamelia's mum believes she is coping with parenting her children, what she believes her strengths and weaknesses might be and whether, as a responsible parent, she might wish to do things differently.

In my experience, sensitive but focused discussion with Jamelia's mum should lead you to be able to make an assessment as to what should happen next. As detailed in Chapter 4, this should follow discussion with the Designated Person for Safeguarding and careful plotting of the risk, harm and need factors, in relation to strengths and protective factors, using the scales model.

- If Jamelia's mum is willing to talk with you about information provided by the health visitor, acts favourably to discussion about the family's history, including the death of the baby and Jamelia's health needs, this would add further weight to the strengths and protection factors side of the scales model.

Example: Working effectively as a 'team around the child'

– If she refused to engage with the key person, denied, disputed or minimised these aspects of professional concern, however, this would add weight to the risk, harm and need factors side of the scales model.

Whatever the case, as you will have discussed in your practitioner team while looking at this case study, it will be necessary to co-ordinate a multi-professional response to Jamelia's needs and those of her wider family. Jamelia's mum's level of engagement with the key person, possibly along with the designated person or manager, will also help to determine whether the response should be at the formal targeted intervention level – including beginning a CAF – Section 17 of CA 1989 applies here. (Take a look at the wording of key parts of CA 1989, at the end of this chapter. This will help you to identify which parts of CA 1989 apply.)

Your view may be that professional concern has reached a serious level, which would be understood as *child protection*. This level of concern might be satisfied if, for example, Jamelia's mum actively refutes that her daughter has *any*

health care needs, suggests that her needs are brought about by her being a 'bad or possessed child' (which might also indicate that the parent has a mental health need). In this case CA 1989, Section 31 (9) would apply (The wording for this part of the Act can be found at the end of this chapter).

Whatever the case, as discussed in previous chapters it is of vital importance that practitioners recognise their responsibility to:

● Reassure the child's parents and work closely with them in making contact with the wider Children's Services (including Children's Social Care, if appropriate)

● Alert professionals from the wider Children's Services to the need for a 'team around the child' multi-disciplinary approach

● Play a confident part in the 'team around the child' approach, including taking on the lead practitioner role where a CAF is started.

Respect and value each other's professional opinion

Applying the law when working

We are the keepers of current knowledge and we need to own it

Work together

It is both essential that we truly own our professional knowledge as 'the keepers of what is usual growth and development' and assert this with confidence. It is equally important that we respectfully challenge professional practitioners from other disciplines where they express views that are inaccurate, misinformed or skewed in some way. It is vital to keep in mind that social workers, for example, may be informed to a very basic level regarding the usual growth and development of young children. In comparison, this is your area of expertise and it is fully appropriate that you challenge a social worker in their misinformed, naïve opinion, as necessary. They are, after all, mostly experienced in working with complex, distressed, disordered and disorganised relationships and family dynamics and rarely have a vast experience of working with hundreds of three-year-olds.

Dynamics at play in inter-professional working

Confident participation as a full and equal member of the multi-disciplinary professional 'team around the child' requires us to be alert to the kinds of behaviour and interaction that represent effective and collaborative work together. These include actively listening, respecting and valuing each other's

professional opinion, including the knowledge and experience on which it is based. We should be competent in asking for clarity surrounding another professional's area of expertise and confident in challenging another's opinion. We should be able to do this while maintaining our central focus on the child and their family.

There are occasions, however, when professional focus has shifted to competitive, undermining or distracting behaviours. In more extreme cases this behaviour might be accompanied by levels of bullying, including inappropriate use of status or power. In these cases it is essential that these behaviours are exposed, challenged and if necessary taken to higher levels of management for resolution. In this way distraction from the main job in hand, ensuring that effective early help is provided to the child and their family, can be restored.

A final word on inter-professional working: Keeping yourself out of trouble

In the course of training work with early years practitioners, they have often referred to 'gathering evidence' or 'investigating' their concerns for children and their families.

This is dangerous territory. It is the responsibility of Children's Social Care and the Police Child Abuse Investigation Team, our professional partners, to 'gather evidence' and 'conduct investigations'. If we want to be fully respected for the part we play alongside our professional partners, we should be familiar with our own role and responsibilities, in addition to theirs. If you have been using these terms in the course of your work, it is urged that you stop. It will keep you out of trouble!

Applying the law when working with children and their families

The Children Act 1989 and the Children Act 2004 apply when working across the full safeguarding spectrum with children and their families.

The Children Act 2004, Section 11 creates a duty for the key agencies to work with children to put in place arrangements to make sure that they take account of the need to safeguard and promote the welfare of children when doing their jobs.

This means that the childcare provision, and all practitioners who work within it, must work in line with the EYFS Safeguarding and Welfare Requirements. This includes working to:

- *What to do if you're worried a child is being abused* (2006)

- *Working Together to Safeguard Children* (2010, currently under review)

- *Information-sharing: Guidance for practitioners and managers* (2008).

In work with children and parents at the *targeted level of intervention*, the following parts of CA 1989 apply:

Firstly, that all professional services (including child care provision) have a duty to:

> "...safeguard and promote the welfare of children within their area who are in need; and so far as is consistent with that duty, to promote the upbringing of such children by their families, by providing a range and level of services appropriate to those children's needs".
> Children Act 1989, Section 17 (1)

LINKS WITH YOUR PRACTICE

Our shared responsibility to work as equal members of a multi-disciplinary team of practitioners includes:

- Working as a key member of the 'team around the child' or core group (in the case of a child protection plan being in place for a child)

- The importance of being well-informed about the early years' practitioner's role in relation to the professional role of others and to take ownership of this role in equal partnership with others.

- Being mindful in the use of appropriate professional terms and language i.e. practitioners's role to **observe**, **record** and **report**, not 'gather evidence' or 'investigate'

- Exploration of what a truly collaborative and meaningful relationship looks like between professional practitioners and how this is developed in a transparent way in partnership with parents

- Playing a part in joint ownership of an assessment, in **partnership** with the parents, including consideration of risk, harm and need in relation to strengths and protective factors

- Taking proud ownership of our early childhood development knowledge and actively applying it in making the comparison between this child's health and development, as opposed to a 'similar child' CA 1989, Section 31

- Having a clear understanding of how specific sections of CA 1989 apply, according to how the individual features of the child and family present themselves

- Assuming the obligation to grow in professional confidence in such a way to ensure the focus for joint work is upon sharing professional expertise and assessment of the child and their family and not on 'point scoring' between sectors of the Children's Services

- Responsibility to challenge discriminatory, prejudiced or poorly-informed decision-making in the wider professional network, including how breaches to joint work should be raised with senior managers for resolution, as appropriate.

The term "Children in Need" is defined in CA 1989, Section 17 (10): A child shall be taken to be in need if –

(a) He/she is unlikely to achieve or maintain or have the opportunity of achieving or maintaining, a reasonable standard of health or development without the provision for him/her of services by local authority under this part:

(b) His/her health or development is likely to be significantly impaired, or further impaired without the provision for him/her of such services:

(c) He/she is disabled

The descriptions of 'development' and 'health' are given to guide us:

"development" means physical, intellectual, emotional, social or behavioural development

"health" means physical or mental health;

at a **serious level of professional concern**, or **child protection**, the law describes "significant harm". It says:

The Children Act 1989, Section 31 (9) as amended by the Adoption and Children Act 2002, regarding "significant harm" reads:

"Where the question of whether harm suffered by a child is significant turns on the child's health or development, his health or development shall be compared to that which would be reasonably expected of a similar child".

Again, 'harm' and 'ill treatment' are described, to guide us:

"'Harm' means ill treatment or the impairment of health or development, including, for example, impairment suffered from seeing or hearing the ill treatment of another". (This includes a child being in an environment of domestic abuse. This might include their own home, someone else's or their childminder's home or a group care provision. The child does not need to be in the same room to be affected.)

"'Ill treatment' includes emotional abuse, neglect, physical and sexual abuse".

The same definitions of 'development' and 'health' apply as in Section 17, above.

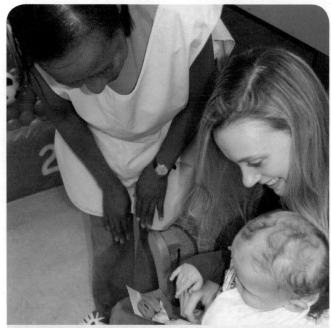

A meaningful relationship between practitioners and parents actively promotes children's protection and welfare

KEY POINTS IN MAKING INTERGRATED WORKING A REALITY: MULTI-AGENCY COLLABORATION

- It is essential that early years practitioners take up their equal membership in all multi-disciplinary work, whether this is a part of the 'team around the child' (with accompanying CAF) or member of a core group (where a child is subject to a child protection plan). It is vital that practitioners are competent to present their professional view with confidence and authority

- Where practitioners do not yet hold sufficient confidence to participate in this way, this must be addressed as a matter of urgency

- Without focus on this development, key information can be lost and the child can be placed at further risk of harm

Chapter 6

Getting the balance right: Rights and responsibilities

In child care environments where there is a genuine interest in becoming artists in human relationships, a deep level of interest and reflection is given to the range of human behaviours and the diverse ways in which they are expressed. This includes an interest in both the behaviours of children and adults, whether they are parents, practitioners within our own provision or those who work in the wider Children's Services.

In the previous chapters we have concentrated much attention on the importance of creating relationships and ways of communicating, that are:

- Committed to keeping the main focus on the child and their family

- 'In step' with an explicitly owned philosophy, approach and culture to child care

- Based on the legal guidance, particularly EYFS, in striving towards high standards

- Mindful of the impact that practitioners have on both the child and their family

- Formally owned as having been guided by practitioners, as opposed to being seen as accidental and random connections between human beings.

A spotlight has also been trained upon the significance of developing an emotionally mature and competent team and the costs of not recognising and acting on clues to professionally toxic relationships. By this I refer to situations where perhaps needy, immature practitioners either knowingly or unknowingly wield their power over children and/or parents. Such practitioners might be unwittingly 'let loose' on children and families that we might recognise as vulnerable by nature of the route by which they arrived at the provision or come to the notice of practitioners as needy at a later date. Whatever the case, where this happens it is clear that there has been a wholly inappropriate use of professional power and those who we are charged with supporting and safeguarding have, in fact, been subject to a harmful influence.

In this chapter we will focus specifically on the importance of defining *how* professionally ethical, competent practitioners enter into and maintain relationships with children and their families. In this we will consider:

- How they operate as a part of a team, whether this is a family supporting the childminder, or a team within a group care provision

- The heavy cost to practitioners, children and families (in the form of complaints and allegations), if we do not work to these principles

- The importance of developing a professional code of conduct for the provision

- What must happen if an allegation is made against a professional practitioner or, in the case of a childminding household, a member of the family unit.

- The legal duty to work in partnership with the local authority designated officer (LADO), Children's Social Care and possibly the Police Child Abuse Investigation Team under the Allegations against Practitioners procedure.

Keeping children safe includes following the building security policy and monitoring all visitors

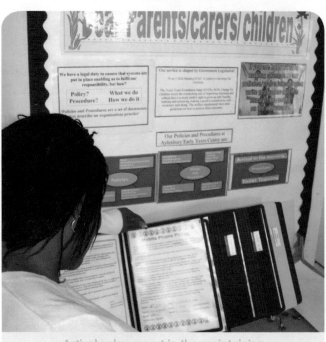

Actively play a part in the maintaining high standards of professional practise

Placing focus on professional practice at a deeper level

In Chapters 1-3, the responsibility for establishing a safe environment for children, their families and practitioners, was explored. The roles of the manager, designated person and registered person have also been subject to consistent reference, in their responsibility to:

- Maintain an objective overview of the team and how well it is functioning

- Devise and implement a provision development plan based on observation, assessment and analysis of professional practice – individually and as a team

- Be vigilant to the relational dynamic between practitioners and children, practitioners and parents, practitioners and managers and practitioners with each other

- Develop the emotional maturity and competence of the workforce

- Make timely managerial interventions where necessary, including use of disciplinary processes.

Whether the provision is a small pre-school group or childminding household, development of the team (or family) is never fully taken care of, i.e. it will always need careful attention. Ensure that strengths are monitored and frictions taken into account on a daily basis. Let's take a look at Angela's approach to setting up 'the rules' for her family and friend network and how important these proved to be when this broke down with her mum.

Initially Angela's mum had been supportive of her daughter's application to childmind. Within a month of Angela setting boundaries with her mum about coming to the house though, she became jealous of the attention Angela was showing towards other families. This escalated quickly and she made a complaint to Ofsted about her daughter. We need to manage the fine balance of relationships every day, including with 'emotionally needy' family members or your team drama queen (we all have one). They need to know that they will receive attention, but never at the expense of diverting attention from your core work with children and their families.

As indicated, it is the manager's (or childminder's), responsibility to manage the emotional environment for children, their parents and each other – in that order. This might include needing to guide a practitioner down the 'capability path' as a part of the wider disciplinary process. A failure to do this can ultimately lead to the kind of situation as described in the Plymouth

Serious Case Review (SCR), where an abusive practitioner can be left unchallenged to:

- Be selective in the kind of relationships she entered into with some children, families and practitioners (favouritism and discriminatory practice)

- Manipulate, 'charm' and groom children and adults alike (the recognised behaviour of sex offenders and others who wish to exploit the vulnerable or divert attention from poor practice)

- Ingratiate themselves with managers and/or disregard managerial guidance

- Disregard policy and procedure

- Do exactly as they wish to do, unchallenged by the wider team (or family). 'K', as she was referred to in the SCR, had the opportunity to take indecent images of babies and then pass them to 'H', who in turn distributed them to a much wider network of sexual offenders.

In my opinion, the message is clear – we cannot afford to be complacent. We cannot trust that, just because a practitioner (or family member) has a cleared CRB check and has been recruited according to safe recruitment procedures, they are 'safe' to work with children. We need to be 'on the ball', consistently questioning and willing to put the provision's whistle-blowing procedure to the test.

So, having reflected on the ways that professionally qualified and 'apparently' safe practitioners might 'mould' and take control, how can we design a provision that could be described as 'vigilant' and therefore reduce the likelihood of abuse happening?

Closing the net on poor and mal practice

In provisions where the risks associated with complacent, naïve or disinterested practice have been recognised, teams have come together to agree exactly what their standards are. My associates and I have facilitated many such events for both childminders and group care practitioner teams. With childminders this has often included the opportunity for partners (such as Angela's husband) to reflect on how they and the wider family unit can really support successful childminding, ensuring that the needs of family members and childminded children and their families can be balanced.

When Angela initially attended the 'Introduction to Childminding' course her family said that they fully supported her. Her husband had attended the first part of the safeguarding course with her six months earlier and said that he intended to do all he could in assisting her to build a career from home (and he was clear that it was a career and not just 'a job' for Angela).

During the course Angela and her husband agreed some 'house rules' for Angela's home-based career. They agreed that they would talk the rules through with their six and nine year old daughters, Angela's friends who had become used to her being around at home and her mum, who lived a few streets away. Angela's 'house rules' and professional Code of Conduct included:

- During 7.30am-6pm, Monday to Friday, 'my home is my office and office-type behaviours apply'. This included no 'popping in' of friends, no TV or rough games, or too grown-up games around the minded children

- Angela, her husband and their daughters being dressed appropriately and behaving appropriately during childminding hours, as well as being mindful as to how they conducted themselves in the community at other times

- Angela having professional boundaries in place with children and parents, to ensure that parents were clear that her approach was 'friendly', but not intending to 'be a friend', offering child care during childminding hours and not extending this to babysitting or socialising together

- Ensuring that Angela's own daughters understood that Angela was the registered childminder, and not them by association. Also, that Angela would be the only one changing nappies, feeding babies and applying the behaviour policy – i.e. it was not the role of her daughters to discipline the children!

- Conducting herself in a professionally confident and assertive manner, including offering advice and support to parents and, where this was declined, that Angela would not lose focus on the child's needs.

POINT FOR REFLECTION

An example of a few elements of a group care provision, Code of Professional Practice

We will:

- Support each other in ensuring that communication between the Key Person and parent is maintained to a high standard (this followed discussion that on occasion practitioners had 'played games' in withholding messages, not giving feed back because they were not the Key Person, or failed to do so because they did not like the Key Person or the parent)

- Talk explicitly with parents about our professional child care role being clearly focused on the child's development, safety, welfare and well-being and offer support and assistance to the parent in being the best parent they can be (this followed discussion that on occasion practitioners had blurred professional boundaries by attending children's birthday parties or naming ceremonies for babies, became god parents and/or socialised with parents, including entering in to sexual and/or romantic relationships)

- Actively support the growth of each other's professional competence and confidence within the team and challenge and actively play a part in maintaining high standards of professional practice (this followed discussion that on occasion the team had been made up of cliques of friends and those excluded from the cliques, competitiveness, bitchiness and purposely undermining behaviours)

- Aim to support professionally reflective practice, play our part in expanding ourselves and accept managerial guidance and support in a mature way (this followed discussion that on occasion practitioners had responded to managerial guidance as interfering, threatening and critical in a negative way and as a consequence had gossiped with colleagues, resisted being managed and refused to attend training)

- Be mindful of the personal attitudes, beliefs and values that we bring into the workplace (this followed discussion that religious, cultural and political views had been discriminatory).

During these events we often pause to consider how childminders' own children and partners may become resentful or jealous of the minded children, due to their mum/dad or partner giving time to others in their home. We spend quality time unpicking perfectly natural human behaviour, particularly for the childminder's son – who at 2½ years, might not always wants to share his mum, his toys and his house. We look at the attitudes, behaviour and conduct of both 'safer/ reflective' practitioners and 'risky/dangerous' practitioners and their supporting team, whether this is the wider family and friend network, as in Angela's case, or the wider provision practitioner team.

During this reflection process teams are able to agree the structure and content of a professional code of practice or conduct. Because everyone contributes to this process, the resulting code of conduct is jointly owned. This then provides the framework against which practitioners continue to conduct themselves, challenge each other and expect to be managed. This process of creating and then regularly reviewing the code of professional conduct links closely with creating (and reviewing) values and philosophy as outlined in Chapter 2.

It is essential that all practitioners are fully accountable for what happens in their environment

- With children

Design and adopt a code of professional conduct across the team or childminding household

- With their parents

- With their practitioner team

- With the management and leadership provided

- In the dynamics between all parties.

This includes being accountable for providing a properly child-focused provision, providing meaningful partnership with children's parents, working in an ethical and supportive way with each other within the team and with the wider Children's Services...and subsequently, delivering this in a consistently competent and confident manner.

This also includes professional practitioners being aware of the power, control and influence that they can have over children and families, and taking responsibility not to use this power or influence to harmful effect. Professionally harmful behaviour might include making value judgements, and sharing these as factual statements which may then assume 'truthful' status.

It is our role to censor ourselves in a professionally reflective way, protect high professional standards and be prepared to be a lone voice in expressing concern. In making this journey we may well discover fellow practitioners whose motivation in doing the job they do, or in the actions they may take, lead us to question those motivations.

On occasions, this might include practitioners witnessing active abuse of children, parents or the manipulation of fellow practitioners, including hearing of such accounts. (Similar to to those described in the Plymouth Serious Case Review.)

Being 'alive' to the possibility that allegations against practitioners can and do arise

It is essential to remember that adults who abuse children physically, emotionally, psychologically, sexually or through neglecting them, can achieve very easy access to both children and socially vulnerable parents in an early years provision. Such abuse might be actively intended or unintentional (i.e. be a manifestation of the practitioner's emotional immaturity). These practitioners, both men and women, may arrive at the provision with excellent references, high professional credibility and cleared checks.

Indeed, the Plymouth SCR challenged all of our professional stereo-types and dispelled myths about who sexually abuses children. The practitioner 'K':

- Was a heterosexual woman, married with children herself

- Held a professional child care qualification

- Had been CRB checked.

As discussed in earlier chapters, it is important that we recognise that practitioners working within early years provision, do, on occasion, carry a history of abuse from their own upbringing or were otherwise affected by events in their own childhood. Practitioners may be affected in an enduring way by these past events in their adult life and may equally be involved in abusive relationships currently. Such practitioners may be more vulnerable to being manipulated by both abusive parents or practitioners, reduced in their capacity to identify harm in children or may actively harm children and or parents. Managers should therefore actively encourage appropriate disclosure of such history, personal experience and current circumstances and assist practitioners in their professional growth and development in an appropriate way. It is, however, the manager's role to undertake a sensitive assessment in partnership with the practitioner in establishing whether these abuse experiences are so obscured from view that they cannot be handled in a reliable way, or whether the practitioner can contain themselves and their emotional responses. It is important to stress that the child care provision is not a therapeutic, rehabilitation opportunity for practitioners, but should be an environment where young children and their families receive warm, nurturing care and education. It is equally vital for the manager to own their responsibility to:

- Assess the emotional/psychological fitness of the practitioner

- Put appropriate measures in place to manage the practitioner's welfare (this might include offering support in access to counselling services)

- Assist the practitioner in appropriate emotional self-management through professional supervision

- Counsel the practitioner out of the profession, should their emotional fitness be insufficiently robust to provide consistent, reliable and nurturing care to young children.

Having established the firm, emotionally mature foundations on which all child care should be based, (as identified in Chapter 3), it is essential that all practitioners read, understand and work to the provision's safeguarding children policy and procedure, including the code of professional practice. This forms the basis on which all practitioners are employed, i.e. the provision philosophy, working culture, daily routine, policies and procedures which all relate to the legal contract agreed with the employer. Failure to work to this guidance is therefore essentially breaking the employment contract.

Recognising allegations or complaints

Up to 65-70% of allegations or complaints could be potentially avoided if the principles for high professional standards in practice, outlined in this book, are followed. This includes:

- Practitioners entering into confident, open communication with children and their families daily

- Developing a provision philosophy and culture where children, families, members of the immediate community and practitioners from the wider Children's Services, can share information and concerns freely and without prejudice

- All parties being familiar with both the whistle-blowing and allegations against practitioners procedure.

The allegations against practitioner's procedure must be written according to the guidance laid out in the *Working Together to Safeguard Children* (2010, Appendix 5, currently under review) and guidance issued by the Safeguarding Children Board within the area that the childminder or group care provision is located. This procedure must include what a practitioner team or management committee should do if an allegation is made against a manager.

It is vital that the procedure emphasises the wide array of ways in which allegations might come to the practitioner's attention, i.e. through an overheard conversation, in direct form by a child, a group of children or a parent, through other practitioners, from neighbours to the provision, or via professional practitioners from a range of other services. It is important to recognise that the allegation may be made in response to a recent event or an event that occurred some time ago. Whatever the specific nature, timing or source of the allegation, it must be taken seriously.

In some circumstances the provision may only become aware that an allegation has been made when they are contacted by either Children's Social Care or by Ofsted. This might relate to a practitioner being the subject of an investigation regarding the care of:

- Children within the provision

- The practitioner's own children

- Children in another setting, e.g. faith setting, youth or arts project.

In all circumstances the formal allegations against practitioners, child protection procedure applies.

The registered person for the provision should be informed of the allegation against the practitioner as soon as possible. This is essential as they have a legal duty to:

- Ensure that the safeguarding responsibility toward the child or children concerned, is followed

- Protect and safeguard all children and vulnerable parents within the provision

- Ensure their duty of care towards the practitioner against whom the allegation has been made, is managed, as a 'reasonable employer'

- Co-operate with Children's Social Care, the Police Child Abuse Investigation Team and Ofsted as necessary and appropriate.

Where the allegation has been made against the registered person, the provision's procedure should clearly identify who is responsible for leading the process.

Under no circumstances should allegations be minimised or ignored.

Acting on allegations against practitioners: the procedure

Whether the allegation has been made against a practitioner who is employed directly by the provision, via an employment agency or is a student or trainee with a college, academy or secondary school, the following steps must be followed.

Listening carefully to the person making the allegation may reveal a simple explanation

Maintaining a regular dialogue with parents also helps to reduce the likelihood of 'niggles' in the relationship

1. The registered person (in most cases the manager), should gather basic information regarding the allegation. (It should be remembered that the role is to gather information, but *not* to investigate.) This stage should include talking with the person who received the initial allegation or witnessed the harm and/or talking to the person who made the allegation, themselves. This part of the process should be conducted using open-ended questions, in order not 'to lead or influence' what is being said in any way. Clarity should be reached about what was alleged to have happened, where it happened, who was involved, who might have witnessed this and what has been said by the first person to have received the allegation. The manager should make detailed notes for their own use, but not take statements or ask anyone giving information, to sign notes. (This is the role of the Police Child Abuse Investigation Team.) The registered person may contact the LADO within the borough or authority within which their provision is based, for guidance and support.

(The importance of this part of the process cannot over-emphasised. Careful information gathering at this stage will often reveal a simple misunderstanding or conflict between people that might be easily resolved through a facilitated discussion. In this case moving on to step 2 may not be necessary or appropriate.)

2. The LADO should be contacted within one day of the allegation being received. In discussion with the LADO it should be agreed what needs to happen next, by whom and within what timescale. Advice received from the LADO should be followed as their role is one where they frequently give advice to a range of child care provision. They will guide the registered person through the legal procedure and they may be aware of prior information regarding the person against whom the allegation has been made. It is also advisable to inform Ofsted of the allegation at this point, but the regulating body should certainly be contacted within fourteen days.

(At this stage it may become clear that the allegation is not one that should be investigated through the child protection procedures, but is a practitioner conduct matter that should be processed via the provision's disciplinary procedure.)

It is essential registered persons (including childminders) note that this decision is made by Children's Social Care, including the LADO and *not* the provision.

Working Together to Safeguard Children (2010, Appendix 5, currently under review) guides the situations in which the threshold for investigation is met. The guidance says:

Share information and concerns
freely and without prejudice

"The framework for managing cases set out in this guidance applies to a wider range of allegations than those in which there is reasonable cause to believe a child is suffering, or is likely to suffer, significant harm. It also caters for cases of allegations that might indicate that s/he is unsuitable to continue to work with children in their present position, or in any capacity. It should be used in respect of all cases in which it is alleged that a person who works with children has:

● Behaved in a way that has harmed a child, or may have harmed a child;

● Possibly committed a criminal offence against or related to a child; or

● Behaved towards a child or children in a way that indicates s/he is unsuitable to work with children."

(The guidance refers to this 'wider range of allegations' to cover situations in which practitioners might have acted in an unprofessional way and/or have breached their position of trust with the child and/or parent and may therefore be found to be unsuitable to work with children. This might include, for example, a situation where a practitioner has psychologically bullied a child or handled them roughly, which clearly does not align with nurturing care of children within a professional child care environment.)

3. Where it is agreed that the threshold has been met for an investigation by Children's Social Care and possibly the Police Child Abuse Investigation Team, the process will be guided by them. This often begins with a strategy meeting which the registered person should attend. The purpose of this meeting is to collate relevant information, decide on what should happen next, in what order and who will undertake each task. It is essential that the registered person co-operates fully in this process and seeks guidance as to how aspects of their own disciplinary procedure are to be applied. For example, it may be decided that the practitioner against whom the allegation has been made should be suspended while the investigation is being conducted. The provision's disciplinary procedure should not be applied in full, however, until after the investigation has been confirmed as complete.

4 Although there is clear guidance with regard to how long an investigation should take, investigations vary according to the complexity. There may, for example, be a series of strategy meetings, which the registered person should continue to attend. Throughout the investigation it is important that the practitioner is provided with support, although it is vital that this does not prejudice the investigation. It is also the responsibility of the manager to make an appropriate announcement to the team and keep parents informed (as appropriate), while being mindful of confidentiality and containing reactions to the investigation.

5. The findings of the investigation by Children's Social Care and, if involved, the Police Child Abuse Investigation Team, should be provided to the registered person at the conclusion of the process. It is important to note that this might not provide a conclusive and substantiated outcome that leads to criminal charge. The findings may indicate that children and/or vulnerable parents have been harmed and the action or inaction of the practitioner suggests that they are unsuitable to work with children. In this case the registered person would progress by following their disciplinary procedure, making use of the findings from the investigation. Where there are no conclusive findings to substantiate that abuse to children or vulnerable parents, or poor or mal practice has been found, the process is complete. In this case, appropriate support should be provided to the practitioner in drawing the matter to a close and the findings of the investigation should be entered clearly on the practitioner's personnel file.

6. Where findings from the investigation lead to the full disciplinary procedure being followed, the registered person

should give careful consideration as to the ways in which the practitioner conducted themselves, how far this differed from the expectations of a professional child care practitioner and whether this is at a level where:

- Gross misconduct or misconduct grounds have been met (according to the provision code for professional practice), in which case the decision to terminate the contract might be appropriate

- Misconduct grounds have been met, in which case clear guidance is provided, including a clear plan specifying the development/improvement that needs to be made, within what timescale, when and by whom, this will be reviewed

- Neither misconduct grounds have been met but responsibility for inappropriate practice has been owned by either/both the practitioner and registered person, in which case appropriate guidance, support and if relevant, training, might then be put in place for the practitioner. As detailed in the above scenario, this should include a review date, in order that progress can be monitored.

It should be noted that this range of possible responses, is not intended to be exhaustive. It is presented for illustration purposes only.

7. If the decisions reached during the disciplinary process include either a variation or termination of the practitioner's contract, this must be communicated to:

- The Independent Safeguarding Authority, under the Vetting and Barring Scheme

- Ofsted.

Failure to satisfy these requirements is a criminal offence.

The investigation process for childminding households

As outlined, allegations within the childminding environment might relate to either the childminder themselves, or a member of the wider household. As childminders often work in a 'lone' capacity and *are* the registered person, they are obviously not in a position to manage themselves through the investigation

LINKS WITH YOUR PRACTICE

Highlighting what makes for an emotionally mature and competent team of practitioners, includes:

- Being able to recognise ways in which emotionally immature practice might come to the notice of the practitioner team (or household, in the case of home-based child care)

- Managers owning their responsibilities to assess the emotional/psychological 'fitness' of practitioners and take the necessary steps with the practitioner should they temporarily or permanently present as 'unsuitable' to work with children and vulnerable parents, within a professional child care provision

- Recognising the costs of failing to explicitly name behaviours appropriate and entirely inappropriate to professional practice, in terms of complaints and/or allegations against practitioners

- Owning the fundamental importance of boundaried, professional practice in forming and maintaining relationships with children and their families, working as a member of a team (whether group or home-based) and provision of effective management, guidance and supervision (including within a home setting)

- Noting the benefits of having a professional code of conduct in place for the provision, which sets the framework for professional relationships with children, their parents, each other as practitioners and members of the wider Children's Services

- Embedding a professional culture of reflection, personal censorship and awareness as a whole team (or family)

- Recognising the ways in which complaints or allegations arise, how they should be responded to under the safeguarding umbrella, in line with the child protection legislation and guidance and *not* investigated by the provision manager, or covered up altogether

- Being able to 'learn the lessons' from what the allegation and subsequent investigation, brought to light, including bringing mature 'closure' to the matter for all members of the provision.

process. Whilst the general principles of the procedure outlined in 1-7 above apply, childminders would be expected to:

- Reassure the person making the allegation that it will be taken seriously and managed through the proper procedural channels. (It is important to ensure that the allegation is referred in this way and that the childminder does not stop in taking this action should the person making the allegation wish to withdraw it, 'back track' or change their mind.)

- Inform Ofsted, as the regulating body, at the point that an allegation is made against either themselves or a member of their household. (This is regardless of whether they believe that the allegation is 'true' or not.) N.B. It is an offence not to inform Ofsted of an allegation – this *must be* done within fourteen days

- Inform the Early Years Advisory Team, or Childminding Network Co-ordinator within the borough or local authority within which they work. This service will provide further guidance including making contacts with the LADO and Children's Social Care

- Record what exactly was said at the point the allegation was made, who said it, when and what the childminder and/or other members of the household said in response. It is also important to note the circumstances in which the allegation was made, i.e. did this follow a conflict or longstanding disagreement, what is the emotional or mental health state of the person making the allegation?

- Co-operate fully in the investigation process, as openly and honestly as possible

- Comment on any past or current concerns they have for the child and/or parent, in giving any possible background to the allegation

- Make both past and current records freely available during the investigation process, as these might shed light on what has been a brewing breakdown in relationship or evidence of parental ill mental health, for example

- Follow guidance and advice given, i.e. to not talk to a partner or son or daughter regarding the allegation that has been made, or undertake their own investigation

- Establish whether (if a full and formal investigation is to be carried out), their registration will be suspended, in which case childminded children will not be able to come to the house

- Ensure that communication with childminded children's parents is based on advice from Children's Social Care

- Be mindful to 'contain' professional concern and anxiety regarding the investigation process in an appropriate way for both themselves and their wider family, i.e. not get emotionally charged or talk to anyone and everyone in an unboundaried way.

Guidance and support can also be sought via the NCMA and/ or a solicitor. It may be useful to have trusted childminder colleagues prepared to offer support to each other, in advance of the need to request it.

Allegations against practitioners, whether within a group care or household environment, can be distressing, not only for the practitioner (or family member) concerned, but for the wider team. It is essential that the process, once complete, is brought to a well-managed 'closure'. This will include making an appropriate statement about the outcomes and taking the learning from the process into development of the team's (or childminding family's) practice. This pause for reflection is essential, as it potentially sets the tone for the quality of all future child care.

KEY POINTS IN GETTING THE BALANCE RIGHT: RIGHTS AND RESPONSIBILITIES

- High standards in professional conduct and behaviour are fundamental to excellence in childcare provision

- These are reflected in practitioners being emotionally available in a consistent way, in order to build relationships with children, parents and their fellow practitioners; practitioners being emotionally mature in both individual and team-working practice, whether this is within a home-based or group care provision; and practitioners actively demonstrating their 'suitability' to work within the child care profession

- Every practitioner has a legal duty to whistle-blow on poor professional standards in child care and to ensure allegations against practitioners are referred through child protection procedures

Chapter 7

Effective leadership and management in safeguarding children

"Be the change you want to see in the world" Mahatma Gandhi.

The mark of great leaders and managers is that they model exactly what they want to see in their teams, they cause others to be accountable for their actions and are not afraid to be unpopular at times. Whether your early years provision is home-based or group care, you need a manager who will provide clear leadership in high quality, safe, nurturing care for children and their families. In the case of the childminding household, this person is naturally the childminder, as the registered person. In this chapter, a number of key themes from this book will be drawn together, to focus on the accountabilities of a leader and manager, including:

- Specifying what the leadership and management role entails

- Owning a vision and philosophy for the provision and translating it into practice

- Providing the framework to facilitate both individual and team (or family), growth and development

- Evolving the designated person role

- Managing the emotional competence of the team.

Challenging yourself as a leader and manager

As outlined in Chapters 2, 3 and 4, the managerial role is to facilitate the development of practitioners who are artists in human relationships. To succeed in this endeavor the manager has to be competent in creating a meaningful partnership with the registered person, proprietor and management committee as relevant. Although in some circumstances these roles will be held by the same person, it is important that all aspects of the roles are fully embraced. Of particular significance is the manager being willing to really own the challenge of leading a team, or for a childminder, their family. Let's take a closer look at what it might take.

Are you willing to:

- Stand up for what you believe in regarding high standard provision to young children and their families?

A leader inspires the vision, philosophy and culture of the provision

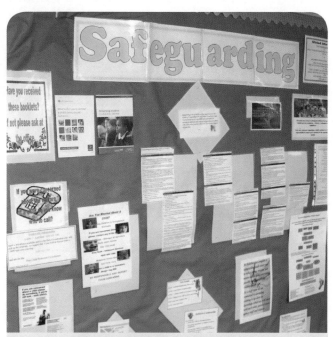

Effective managers provide the tools for practitioners to do their job well

Create meaningful partnerships

- Be the only person to believe in it while you build the team or, for the childminder, get your family and friends fully behind you (as Angela did in Chapter 6)?

- Potentially be unpopular with practitioners who need to be formally 'guided' to improve their practice?

- Be responsible for building on your own professional confidence, in order that the wider team can stand on your firm foundations?

- Be known as an inspiring, innovative leader?

- Never be recognised for the difference that you made for many children, families and practitioners?

It is a pretty tall order, isn't it? What I see in many great leaders and managers is a willingness to 'take themselves on', stretch beyond what they thought was possible and to proudly own the huge importance of what they are doing – not be consumed by their own self-importance. The manager of Stars of Hope nursery put it this way "It's a very personal thing, but I usually know if I am doing the right thing as a manager, if I am feeling afraid. It reminds me that I am challenging myself".

It is important to recognise that a manager does not just 'morph' into a manager overnight. They invariably move into the role following a number of years' experience as a child care practitioner. If they are to grow and develop as a manager, however, it is necessary for them to make investment in their own journey. Through making this commitment to yourself as a leader and manager, you can come to refine your own philosophy for the provision, provide clarity for the team (or family unit) and own your professional authority with confidence.

The complexity of the management and leadership role

The role within most early years provision is complicated and includes up to three quite distinct elements, all of which closely inter-relate – leadership – management – business ownership.

A **leader** inspires the vision, philosophy and culture of the provision and motivates the wider team in translating it into practice.

A **manager** conducts the operations of the provision and ensures that the infrastructure and administrative processes are in place to provide a high quality service, according to the requirements of the law.

A **business owner** provides a service to children and their families for financial profit and seeks to build a reputation in the community with view to attracting an ongoing demand.

Bringing all three elements together in a coherent fashion can be demanding. Although the EYFS allows a great deal of room for individual leader, business owner and manager interpretation, as a regulated service we are required to function within the requirements of the law. This includes:

- Acting as a 'reasonable employer' in the way that practitioners are recruited and selected, supported in fulfilling their professional role, guided, managed and if necessary, disciplined including terminating contacts

- Ensuring that the interface between high quality child care standards and professional conduct and behaviour is established and maintained

- Setting the standards for professionally mature behaviour within the provision and building on the emotional competence of the workforce

- Embedding policy and procedure within the day-to-day functions of the provision in a way that actively demonstrates practitioner ownership

- Instilling a clear culture of professional accountability, where safeguarding children and their families is embraced as a core responsibility by everyone

- Delivering an early years curriculum that inspires practitioners, is accessible and exciting to all children and is understood and supported by parents.

It is the manager's responsibility to ensure that the resources, administrative processes and basic routines are in place in order for the provision to run smoothly. These provide the structure for practitioners to deliver high quality, nurturing care for children and their families. The skill of the manager is to enable and empower practitioners to work within this structure, initially with quite a great deal of close 'on the floor' supervision and guidance. The ultimate goal however is for professionally competent practitioners to take responsibility for their own actions and to self-manage, i.e. to be fully accountable for everything that they do and do not do, to provide explanation for their actions with confidence and to record their decisions accurately.

As we consider the safeguarding-specific responsibilities within the provision, it is essential that a vision has been created for the development of the team, or in the case of the childminder, family unit. Whether the manager holds the designated person for safeguarding role themselves, or supports another practitioner in the role, it is important that there is a plan in place to focus the leadership team in the actions that need to be taken for ongoing incremental development of the team.

Development of the Designated Person

As outlined in Chapter 4, the Designated Person for Safeguarding children need not necessarily hold a managerial position within the group care provision. What is vital, however, is that they hold sufficient authority and status to influence change as necessary and appropriate, in exactly the same way as practitioners working from their home environment must exercise an authority within their own household (as outlined in Angela's case study in Chapter 6).

The fundamental elements of the Designated Person role and the key responsibilities associated with it are laid out in Chapter 4. At a more sophisticated level however, the Designated Person needs to be committed to a consistently evolving model for practice to ensure that the team (or childminding household) is kept in step with modern approaches to work with children and their families. With change to safeguarding practice happening at such a fast pace on both a national and local level, it is important that the designated person gets access to:

- Safeguarding Children Board update training events within the borough or authority that they are located. This should include briefings on the learning from Serious Case Reviews following child deaths or serious injuries. (Attendance at such events also provides the chance to network with professional practitioners from other disciplines, free of specific focus on particular children and their families.)

- Opportunity to meet with fellow Designated Persons to share practice, gain greater perspective on the role and to receive support in developing themselves within the role

- Professional clinical supervision, which is critical during times that they are working with particularly challenging family dynamics.

It is vital that the Designated Person for Safeguarding is able to adopt an objective overview for the entire provision and has the skills to interpret, assess and analyse what they observe. On occasions this might include observations of the practitioner/family member relationship having become blurred, thus distorting objective assessment. As discussed in Chapter 6, this might arise where a practitioner or family member (in the case of a childminding household), disregards the provision's professional code of conduct. This might occur in an innocent way, where a practitioner has become emotionally over-involved on a partially conscious or completely unconscious level. What has been described as a magnetic-like pull of the practitioner towards the child and/or the family, might be due to a number of factors. These might include the practitioner's own early life history, such as abuse and neglect, or even current domestic abuse within their personal relationships. Up until this point the impact of these experiences might have been dormant, buried barely beneath the surface or known and in usual circumstances, contained. Whatever the specific presenting features however, they will need sensitive, careful management by a skillful designated person, working in close partnership with the manager of the provision. It is therefore vital that the designated person has the requisite skills for this role, including well-honed communication skills, capacity to reflect carefully and consider multi-dimensional relationship dynamics and be pro-active in seeking appropriate professional support for themselves. It is equally important that the designated person remains boundaried and clearly distinguishes between their central focus on the safety and welfare of the child and their family, while also exercising their responsibility towards the practitioner, as a 'reasonable employer'.

Managing the emotional competence of the team

As discussed in Chapter 6, it is essential that the leadership team has clear expectations with regard to practitioners' professional conduct and behaviour, both within the provision and outside work hours. In most cases this will be reflected in the code of professional conduct, to which all practitioners (or family members) will have signed up. A key responsibility for the Designated Person then is to assume an objective overview on the interplay of relationship between practitioners, children and their parents. In doing this their role is to monitor the emotional maturity and competence within the workforce and to lead in its ongoing development.

(This section continues on page 77)

LINKS WITH YOUR PRACTICE

Leadership and management in providing high standards of professional emotional competence across the full range of safeguarding responsibilities, includes an ongoing commitment to 'striving for excellence'. It entails:

- The Registered Person (whether a childminder or manager/proprietor of group care), holding a clear vision for the provision and management of the team (or family) in fulfilling on it

- Being bold and courageous in modeling high quality for child care, including safeguarding practice, stretching the team in their respective roles and making all the practical resources available to enable professional growth and development

- Juggling a coherent interface between being a leader, manager and business owner

- Owning the role with an appropriate authority and accountability, reflected in the expectations for professional competence and confidence of practitioners to work in an open, transparent way with children's parents as and when safeguarding concerns arise

- Assuming a clear responsibility for managing practitioners who present as emotionally immature and in some circumstances, actively dangerous in their professional role. This includes the capacity to sensitively manage the practitioner through the competency and/or disciplinary process

- Facilitating the incremental progression of the Designated Person for Safeguarding role, including ensuring that the person holding this role is able to adopt an independent overview of safeguarding practice across the entire provision and has the skills to interpret, assess and analyse what they observe

- Conducting regular and honest assessment and appraisal of the provision, including recognition of strengths and weaknesses, designing a unit plan for development and holding a constantly evolving model in mind for continued progression and enhancement.

Example: Always reaching for excellence

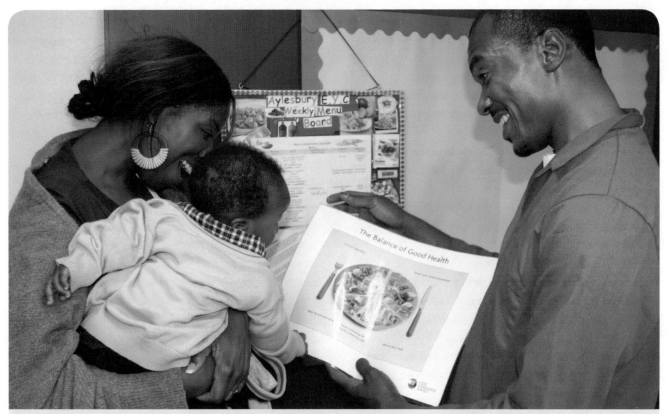

Uncompromising in high quality service to young children

This is what practitioners from a London Early Years Centre had to say about their manager:

"She provides complete clarity and vision. We know exactly what the standards are and what she expects from us".

What distinguishes this manager from many others is that she owns her authority with a quiet confidence and is uncompromising in her stand for high quality service to young children and their families.

The philosophy for the provision is simple, but clear. Practitioners are signed up to it and own it as their own. 'Honest open and truthful communication with everyone'.

The same philosophy extends to working together with the broader Children's Services network. A child and family receiving a priority placement at the provision, for example, will not be allowed to formally take up the place until the parents, social worker, the child's key worker and manager have met together. This way, the manager says "we have agreed the parameters for our work together right from the beginning. This

includes both our approach to work with all children and their families, and our specific approach to work with *this* family. So, if in our work with a child subject to a child protection plan, the parent complains to the social worker that the child is not allowed into nursery as he has diarrhoea, the social worker can say that he recalls us talking about excluding children for 48 hours after the infection has cleared". In a similar way, parents tend to feel less aggrieved if the nursery contacts the social worker each time the child does not come to nursery, because this was discussed in an honest, up front way, right from the beginning. Starting out with these clear boundaries in place assists parents in seeing that close 'team around the child' working is not practitioners being personally nasty to them, but intended to support them in meeting their child's needs more effectively. This consistency and clarity in practice, as discussed in previous chapters, sets the foundations for everyone's growth and development.

- It is made clear to the parents that the practitioners are ready to build a partnership with them in achieving meaningful change in their parenting of their child, according to the details set out in the child protection plan

Example: Always reaching for excellence

- It guides expectations of practitioners across the professional disciplines, i.e. specifying who is going to do what and when

- It establishes 'the rules' for engagement, as outlined in Chapter 6 with regards to practitioners' relationship with the parents, i.e. 'we are friendly, but *not* your friend'

- It keeps central focus firmly on the child, with an emphasis on them being supported to reach their full potential.

The obvious collaboration across the full practitioner team and management team has not happened by accident. Their success, without question, is attributed to:

- The manager delivering a consistent message over the last twelve years and the philosophy and vision being reflected in all written documentation and the whole team 'owning' it

- Consistent focus on the fine detail of practice, each and every day, regular reflection and personal accountability for the standards.

When I met the team to unpick the building blocks to their success, we talked in small sub-teams of two, three of four practitioners at a time. I met with the child care practitioners, the cook and kitchen assistant and the management team. Although I have known practitioners within this team for some time, it has only ever been in a professional capacity as a trainer, when we have met on the three-part safeguarding module I lead or on team-based training, commissioned by the manager. There was ample opportunity for dissenting views to come to the surface, for little niggles or complaints to emerge, but they did not. I left the centre feeling really confident that I could cut through a sub-section of this provision's relationships, whether at an individual practitioner level or collective team level with children, their parents and each other including the management team and the wider professional Children's Services and see exactly the same pattern – 'Honest, open and truthful communication with everyone'.

Can you lay your hand on your heart and say this of your provision?

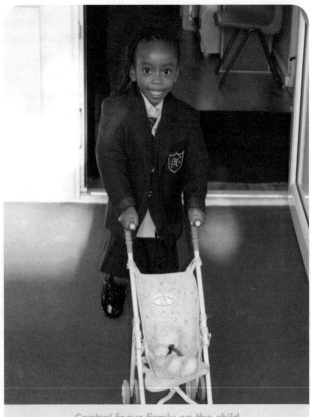

Central focus firmly on the child

Owning the nursery philosophy and vision

What does it mean exactly? Although practitioners are all adults by nature of their chronological age, they differ enormously according to their emotional maturity and capacity to conduct themselves in a professionally competent and responsible way. For example, a forty-year-old practitioner may actually conduct themselves in a way more akin to a thirteen-year-old girl around a crying baby. Where we would expect the practitioner to calmly work through the variety of possible explanations for the baby's cries in attempt to soothe them, the thirteen-year-old girl may approach attempts to soothe the baby in a more random way, perhaps becoming quite agitated by the crying and potentially being distracted by a message from a friend on her iPhone. If the thirteen-year-old kind of behaviours are noted in the forty-year-old practitioner and she gets distracted by her friend while the baby is left to get increasingly distressed, we would question the emotional competence of the practitioner. Naturally it would be necessary to assess whether this was usual conduct for this practitioner, the circumstances during which they might be emotionally unavailable to children and the frequency with which this might happen. This assessment would help to inform the 'next steps' in the management of the practitioner.

Throughout this process the Designated Person and manager need to be clearly focused on their primary responsibility – to provide high quality, nurturing care for children and their families. It is therefore essential that they own their professional responsibility to assess whether the practitioner is so absorbed in his/her own emotional state that they are unable to fulfill their professional role. Indeed it should be recognised that failing to:

a. Identify the need for such an assessment; and

b. Act on the findings, which 'may include' the practitioner posing a risk to the stability, security and safety of the childcare provision;

would be seen as an institutional emotional abuse and/or neglect in itself. In this case it would be necessary to follow the matter up through the practitioner capability route, under the provision disciplinary procedure.

To conclude then, it is the responsibility of the Designated Person to lead the development of the practitioner team in close collaboration with the manager. The development plan should be based on their observation, assessment and analysis of professional practice, both as individuals and as a team. Essential to success in fulfilling the role is the capacity of the designated person to be vigilant to the relational dynamic at all times,

being supportive and encouraging of practice development, while also being decisive in making swift intervention where necessary. Specific focus should be consistently upon supporting professional development, emotional maturity and competence. Specific intervention aimed at supporting development of emotional maturity and competence might include:

- Acting as a role model in providing clarity and discipline for a team as to what is and is not appropriate emotional conduct around children and their families

- Evolving a strategy for individual practitioner and whole practitioner team training and professional development

- Providing emotional 'containment' for both individual practitioners and the practitioner team when particularly challenging child protection concerns arise

- Developing tailored supervision support to practitioners in exploring the development of their emotional competence

- Designing a clear development plan, where the designated person and manager intervention might have reached a formal disciplinary stage with a practitioner

- Facilitating referral and access to professional therapeutic support or counseling.

KEY POINTS IN EFFECTIVE LEADERSHIP AND MANAGEMENT IN SAFEGUARDING CHILDREN

Effective leadership and management includes confident management of practitioners who present as:

- Not yet competent to fulfill their professional role, despite their qualification

- Emotionally unavailable, or immature to form appropriate relationships

- Professionally dangerous in the ways that they conduct themselves

– whether within a home-based or group care environment

Chapter 8

Systems to support the well-being of the provision

There is a stage at which practitioners reach a level of both competence and complete confidence in what they do each and every day. At this stage safeguarding has been so thoroughly integrated into their everyday being that they:

- Operate with an inbuilt radar for picking up actual and/or potential threats, risks and conflict within the child care environment and see it as their responsibility to intervene

- Have a comprehensive understanding of their safeguarding responsibilities across the entire safeguarding spectrum, from early interventions with children and their families, through to following-up on child protection matters

- Are professionally reflective, capable of assessing and analysing their own practice, are prepared for supervision and value the opportunity to view approaches to work with children and families from different perspectives

- Naturally look out for their colleagues, play a key part in their maintaining safe practices and see it as their role to contribute to each others' development

An early years environment is a learning environment for all

Contribute to each others' development

● Are able to view professional practice in an objective way and challenge colleagues both within the provision and wider children's services with a self-assurance

● Have assumed accountability for their own practice and that of others, taking responsibility for mistakes or errors of judgement and practically manage themselves, including confidently informing their manager of matters as appropriate.

In this chapter the structures and processes which support the development of professional competence and confidence to this strong functioning level will be explored in greater depth. The intention, at this stage of the journey, is to draw a number of threads together, with specific focus on the ongoing development of the provision and all practitioners who work within it. This will include:

● Operating as a 'learning provision' which reflects an ongoing commitment to growth and development for all

● Embedding professional learning

● Safer recruitment and selection

● Professional appraisal and supervision.

Providing the framework for development: Walking the talk

It is essential that sufficient resources are allocated to develop the provision, whether this is home-based, led by a lone childminder, or a group care environment. For example, I refer to both the allocation of funds and time set aside to attend training courses. Such opportunities should afford practitioners sufficient head space to fully participate, reflect and consider how they might integrate their learning into practice.

To demonstrate this, the brief case study about Angela in Chapter 6, described that right from the early stages of attending the 'Introduction to Childminding Practice' course, she had sought to involve her family as appropriate. Although individual childminders approach childminding from a range of different perspectives, the way in which Angela had laid the foundations with her husband and daughters not only set up a support structure when she found herself challenged by her mum, but also stood her in good stead when she attended frequent training events at the weekend.

So at the point that Angela needed to deal with her mum's quite jealous reactions to her childminding, Angela had support around her, both from her husband and from other childminders, who had encountered similar situations. In fact, Angela reflected that it could have been easy to throw up her hands in exasperation, complain bitterly and withdraw from childminding, defeated. Apparently this had happened many times before, when she had attempted to launch out, independent of her mum.

This capacity to cope with adversity and bounce back is what Gilligan, Daniel and Wassell (Gilligan R, Daniel B, Wassell S, 1999) refer to as resilience. This capacity or ability is very important in practitioners, as it naturally applies to any relationship, whether this is work with a parent whose behaviour might be quite unpredictable as a result of mental health needs, or joint work with a colleague who might react negatively to making changes to practice. In a progressive provision committed to ongoing development, however, where 'growing people' is obviously a core value to the philosophy, we will see evidence in day-to-day practice.

Learning from Serious Case Reviews

A number of the provisions that I have featured in this book have understood their safeguarding responsibilities in their widest sense for some time. They employ an ongoing commitment to challenging their own attitudes and refining their practice. Over the last years this has included making a detailed, comprehensive response to the messages from the Plymouth Serious Case Review (SCR). This SCR specifically drew attention to the features of a 'safer organisational culture' and referred to this type of environment being much less likely to attract, provide sanctuary and accommodate a risky or dangerous practitioner, such as Vanessa George, without challenge. The SCR refers to: "All those working within Early Years settings as well as those responsible for support and inspection must be mindful of the need for organisations to:

● Operate safer recruitment procedures, including value-based interviewing

● Have effective policies and procedures in place which are communicated to staff, including child protection and intimate care

(This section continues on page 82)

Example: Building a team, fit for purpose

The Zoom approach is clear about its philosophy and values warm, nurturing relationships

Zoom Nurseries is a small south London-based chain that has built a reputation for high quality, nurturing care for children, their families *and* their practitioners. The proprietors have steadily grown their business in the same way that they grow their practitioners – with respect, encouragement and a sense of fun. The Zoom directors have grown up through the organisation in this way and they personify Zoom values. They recruit practitioners and managers according to safer recruitment policy and what seems common to many practitioners is a certain 'pizzazz'. They describe it as a 'brightness', which is not necessarily related to highly qualified or intellectual practitioners, but more a 'being' that is enthusiastic, creative, 'can do' and resilient.

We have worked together over a number of years and what is noticeable is a clear, incremental approach to 'growing' each individual practitioner and the respective teams, both on a whole provision level and individual room-based, team level. The directors and the managers of the respective provisions are talented in accessing training opportunities via the local authority, early years advisory teams. As an organisation they have also allocated funds each year in order to commission

professional training and development events for all Zoom practitioners and managers. These events are scheduled for the annual training week, during which the provisions are closed. They are arranged during school closure periods in order to cause as little disruption as possible to families. Careful consideration is given to the planning of these events and the subject areas on which they will focus. They are arranged according to:

- Common needs for a number of practitioners across the nurseries

- The need to involve the entire organisation workforce in the development of a new strategy (three years ago this included development of the Zoom Code of Professional Practice, similar to the event described in Chapter 6)

- The need for information input and knowledge update

- Specific focus on skills development (a more recent training event was spent assisting practitioners in recognising their strengths to engage effectively with

Example: Building a team, fit for purpose

parents and further build on these. The day addressed recognition of behaviour patterns which might be described as purposefully unco-operative and focus on development of more assertive, confident approaches in work with these parents).

Zoom makes a clear investment in the training and development of their practitioners and has designed an incremental training pathway which links to the professional competency framework. This has been informed by the (former) CWDC Core Skills guidance and the knowledge, aptitudes and skills necessary for practitioners working within the early years sector.

The training pathway maps the comprehensive territory of practice areas and guides managers and supervisors in the progressive development of practitioners. It addresses the specific expectations of practitioners at different points in their career, integrates how long they might have been qualified and how managers should be able to identify the practitioner demonstrating their knowledge *in practice* within the first three months, six months and one year of commencing work with Zoom. This approach, which emphasises the interface between training and the capacity to translate this into practice daily, links to Zoom's responsibility as a 'reasonable employer' to:

- Fulfill their obligation to provide clear factual guidance on what is expected of the practitioner, particularly where this relates to individual legal duties, as in the case of safeguarding

- Equip practitioners in understanding the philosophy, values and principles of the organisation (from the point of induction and throughout the practitioner's career with the company)

- Clearly set the parameters for accountability in practice, i.e. the standards for professional conduct and behaviour in line with the company code of professional practice (a part of the contractual agreement to which the practitioner is employed)

- Place high quality, nurturing care towards children and their families as the central priority to everything that the practitioner engages in.

The investment that Zoom has made in this evolutionary model stretches throughout the organisation. This has included the development of a partnership between myself and my training associates and Zoom provision managers in the design and facilitation of training events and joint appraisal of the outcomes. Detailed evaluation of both individual practitioner and team engagement in the training process is also used to inform ongoing practice development according to the Kolb learning cycle principles (Kolb DA 1984). This holistic approach embraces different learning styles, capacity and pace for individual practitioners, while maintaining a crystal clear focus on maintaining high standards of professional child care. The Zoom approach to professional supervision and appraisal for all practitioners is equally well integrated and makes up a coherent package to inform a continually developing provision. This consistent approach informs all aspects of both practitioner and provision learning in such a way that it is embedded in day-to-day practices. It is this commitment to consistency, in my opinion, that marks Zoom as a truly 'learning provision'.

High quality, nurturing care for children

- Encourage open discussions among the staff group about good and poor practice and facilitate constructive challenge of each other

- Ensure that safeguarding is openly discussed and staff are aware of the possibility that abuse might happen within their workplace

- Have effective whistle blowing procedures

- Have safeguards in place where boundaries may be blurred through friendship networks amongst staff and parents

- Encourage communication and contact with parents and ensure they are kept well informed about their child's day to day experiences".

(Plymouth Safeguarding Children Board: Overview Report in respect of Nursery Z, March 2010)

Many of the specific 'pointers' for development of a safer organisational culture have been addressed in the earlier chapters of this book. However, safer recruitment practice, professional supervision and appraisal processes deserve a little more attention.

Safer recruitment and selection

As outlined in Chapter 1, the Department of Education provides a porthole for provisions' registered persons, management committees, leaders and managers to access accredited Safer Recruitment and Selection training. The guidance specifies that at least one member of the interview panel should have successfully completed this training and has sufficient authority to influence the entire process.

It is equally essential that sufficient resources are allocated in terms of both funds and time, to ensure rigour. This would naturally include all stages of the process, from the advertisement being placed through to a thorough scrutiny of application forms, formal invitation to applicants for interview and conducting checks such as CRB and following up professional references.

At the interview stage it is vital that the panel is not over-reliant on good professional references, 'clear' CRB checks and a prospective practitioner who comes across confidently,

but employs an approach that 'tests' professional values throughout the process. A robust interview process, that employs a 'value-based approach' as indicated in the recommendations of the Plymouth SCR might include:

- Really 'drilling down' into the way that applicants respond to interview questions, probing for a more comprehensive response if necessary and actively following the discussion to a conclusive point

- Giving focus to the emotional maturity and competence of the practitioner, their capacity to reflect and take responsibility for their ongoing development as an artist in human relationships

- Enquiring into the applicant's experience of successfully engaging in relationships with adults and specifically with emotionally 'needy' parents who may, for example, be reluctant to form a relationship or compete with their child for the practitioner's attention

- Focusing on the provision code of professional conduct and whistle blowing policy and establishing meaningful insight as to how the applicant might react in a situation where a professional colleague is behaving inappropriately

- Encouraging applicants to share their motivation to work within the child care professional, including opportunity for disclosure of their own childhood history of abuse and neglect. (Where such a history is disclosed it would be appropriate to explore the ways in which the applicant has managed this history and how they continue to 'contain' their emotional well-being. This dialogue should assist the panel in assessing the suitability of the applicant for employment.)

Although these suggestions are not intended to provide a prescriptive, all-encompassing approach to value-based interviewing, I do believe that they indicate the depth and range that the process should address. They also provide the opportunity for both the interview panel to showcase their provision in a practical way and for the applicant to gain insight into the professional culture, in assessing whether this is a provision that they would wish to join. Adopting this kind of uncompromising approach at the front door to the provision gives a clear message about the importance that the interviewing panel gives to the influence that practitioners have on young children and their families, during their most formative years.

Induction: Fresh eyes on the provision

Following a successful interview and full clearance of the new practitioner as 'suitable' to work with young children and their families, comes the first day, first week and first month within the provision. Their arrival should be greeted as both an opportunity for the provision and the practitioner to reflect on, and if appropriate, to refresh practice.

It is important to recognise that new practitioners often arrive with fresh eyes to the provision and have some valuable observations to share about the organisational culture (Denison D, 1996). Their perceptions may provide useful insight as to how the provision welcomes new children and families, the relative flexibility of the team to 'allow others in' and how consistently practitioners operate, according to the provision's philosophy.

It is equally important to note that it takes an emotionally mature manager and team to both encourage and hear these reflections as an opportunity and not a criticism.

As outlined in Chapters 1 and 7, the manager or leader has a duty to induct all new practitioners with the support and assistance of the wider team. The manager should ensure that stages in the induction process are thoroughly recorded and that the practitioner's incremental progression is monitored as they settle in.

In provisions where thorough attention is given to human resources processes, as with the example of Zoom Nurseries, the induction procedure will be mapped alongside the wider provision training development plan.

This strategic plan details annual targets for development of both individual practitioners and the whole professional team, whilst maintaining a rolling programme of resources including:

- A comprehensive professional training menu, including qualifying courses

- Regular whole practitioner team meetings

- Room-based planning meetings

- Professional supervision and appraisal.

Supervision, a cornerstone to professional development

As indicated in the EYFS Safeguarding and Welfare Requirements 2012, professional supervision assumes a number of different forms which are both formal and informal in type. Informal examples might include the discussion between practitioners over breakfast, as they discuss the provision's response to encouraging small children's independence around toileting, how they explain these emerging abilities to parents and the 'accidents' that might arise as a result. More formal supervision includes the provision's practices in peer-to-peer observation and the one-to-one professional supervision with a more senior practitioner or manager.

Arrangements for professional supervision vary quite considerably across provisions. It is however essential that they address the main purpose of the supervisory function. These are to:

- Provide professional support in the development of the practitioner, encourage reflection on and the application of appropriate theory to their day-to-day practice with children and families (both in general and with specific children and families)

- Ensure that the accountability function is fulfilled, for example children subject to child protection plans are carefully monitored, the child's parents are showing signs

Professional supervision provides the opportunity for mutual exploration and 'growth time'

of co-operation and change in favour of the child's growth and development and reports for child protection conferences are prepared in a timely manner

- Appraise professional learning, identify learning needs, locate opportunities of both a formal and informal nature to further the practitioner's development and integrate learning from attendance on training events into practice

- Support the development of professional competence and confidence, including the growth of emotional maturity in practice with 'needy' children and parents in particular

- Provide appropriate support and, where necessary, mediation to practitioners where professional disagreement or conflict has arisen in any relationship within the provision

- Discuss specific areas for development with the practitioner in cases where their practice is not meeting the expected professional standards. This might include application of the practitioner competency framework.

For supervision to be meaningful both to the supervisee and supervisor, it is essential that it is regular, uninterrupted, well-structured and focused, recorded and valued as a cornerstone to professional practice. It is equally important that the power differentiation between supervisor and supervisee is addressed

and that this vital opportunity for professional reflection and growth does not become viewed as a *painful process*. Indeed in provisions where supervision is happening successfully, both supervisee and supervisor look forward to their 'growth time' together and value the mutual benefit it provides.

It is important that practitioners and managers both providing and receiving supervision are given the opportunity to attend training courses on the supervisory process. This should then be supported by the development and use of a supervision policy for the provision, written agreements and recording formats. Attendance on training courses focused on supervision should be subject to regular review to ensure that it is facilitating professional growth and development.

Professional reflection for childminders

As childminders work as independent businesses, registered by Ofsted as providers, they have no day-to-day manager with whom they can reflect or be supervised. Peer supervision is, however, a process that a number of childminders have developed for themselves within small regional pockets. In a south London borough for example, the Childminding Network Team set up a system for more accomplished and experienced childminders

The importance of effective teamwork

Support development of confidence

to support recently registered childminders in the first years of child care practice. In the same borough locality-based groups of childminders, of varying sizes, meet frequently to mull over challenges in their practice and receive support. Although this structure does not fulfill all dimensions of the supervisory function identified on the opposite page, it does provide the opportunity for support, reflection and considering these challenges from differing perspectives. Equally, in many regions across the country Childminding Network Co-ordinators, Early Years' Advisory Teams and the NCMA provide this level of support and assistance. This is exactly the kind of support that Angela, the childminder case study referred to in Chapter 6, drew upon.

To close, I choose to document a case study, which draws together a number of strands from this book. It addresses the wide range of our safeguarding responsibilities, highlights the skill of artists in human relationships and emphasises the importance of effective team work. In my opinion this example demonstrates an exemplary standard of professional safeguarding practice.

'It is my business': An example of consistent practice on a team level

Here is a great example of practice. It involves a practitioner team's commitment to:

- Safeguard all children and families within their care

- Apply their safeguarding policy in a fully integrated and consistent way

- Act in unity as a team in upholding the philosophy, policies and procedures of their provision

- Maintain an inclusive environment that actively encourages freedom of speech for all parties

- Empower parents to exercise their right to make representations and complaints

- Promoting community learning.

As a provision that is well-integrated within their community they run a 'baby yoga' session for children and families who have

LINKS WITH YOUR PRACTICE

The structures, resources and processes for supporting truly embedded safeguarding practice highlighted, include:

- Setting aside the financial, time and 'head space' resources to develop and grow both individual practitioners and the entire team (or family), including attendance on training events, taking time out for reflection and investing in professional journals and/or research to keep the provision up to date with modern child care and safeguarding practice and messages from Serious Case Reviews, following child deaths

- Evolving a working model that recognises the strengths, successes, individual and collective capacities and skills within the team (or family, for childminders) and utilises these in building resilience further

- Adopting an approach to organisational learning that is in step with the adult learning cycle (Kolb 1984), including the relationship between experiential learning, the opportunity to apply learning to practice and then evaluate practice in applying the learning (i.e. making change to practice 'concrete')

- Making active use of both National and local specialist resources to assist in the continual progression and development of specific aspects of the provision's practice, including, for example, the DfE guidance on Safer Recruitment and Selection, local Safeguarding Children Board protocols etc.

- Being in the constant state of 'life long learning' as a provision, including being open to hearing the reflections and first impressions of parents, visiting professionals and new practitioners to the provision

- Creating and installing a comprehensive model for professional supervision and appraisal, including the use of Childminding Network Forums for home-based practitioners

- Recognising when you have reached a 'state of Nirvana'– in which each and every practitioner, regardless of their professional role or designation, truly owns their legal safeguarding duty, fulfills it, reflects on it and takes responsibility for errors.

places within the nursery and on a drop-in basis, for families in the area. At the beginning of the session one of the practitioners facilitating the session outlines the ground-rules for parents. This includes basic health and safety principles and observing the nursery's policies and procedures, including safeguarding children, parents and practitioners.

On the morning in question a parent took a call on her mobile phone and became irritated when a practitioner encouraged her to take the call outside the room. The emotional heat rose further as another practitioner, supporting the first, quietly asked the parent to leave the room as mobile phones were not permitted in the nursery. The two practitioners made all attempts to invite the parent to end her call or leave the building. In response the parent said, "Don't tell me what to do. You can't control my life".

In an attempt to diffuse the situation, one of the practitioners quietly acknowledged that the parent was angry, said that she was sorry, but that she really needed to leave the room with her phone. (The practitioner explained that her main objective at this stage was to contain the upset and reduce the level of disruption to other babies and parents who by this time seemed anxious. She also said that she was aware that the parent on her phone appeared to have moved into another emotional gear and seemed to be enjoying her audience.) The parent became very agitated, said that she felt that she was being victimised and said that she wished to make a complaint. At this stage, outside the room (with the yoga teacher continuing to lead the session), both practitioners calmly heard her concerns and responded by saying that she could indeed make a formal complaint.

While one practitioner physically pulled back from the conversation with the parent, the other accompanied the parent to the manager's office and briefly explained to the manager that the parent was upset that she had been unable to use her phone in the nursery. The practitioner said that she waited a moment and then, based on her judgement, felt it best to leave the parent to talk with the manager alone. The practitioner explained that she did wait a few minutes, close to the manager's door, just to check that the emotional temperature of the earlier exchange was cooling. As she left the office the practitioner told me that the parent said "You're a grass".

Meanwhile, back in the yoga class, the other practitioner had returned to reassure the other parents and then at the end of the class, had entered into a full explanation as to why neither parents nor practitioners were permitted to use their mobile phones within the nursery. She said that the learning

for the group was extensive and they pieced together some of the messages from the Plymouth Serious Case Review. This included the explicit reference to the way that Vanessa George had used her mobile phone to take indecent images of young children and pass them for wider distribution to a ring of other sexual offenders. This, she explained to the parents, had led to the practitioner team developing tighter guidance regarding the use of digital technology and social media, including the display of notices throughout the building.

The learning for the parent with the phone, by all accounts, was equally great. She had entered into quite a detailed discussion with the manager about her reactions when she perceived that someone was telling her what to do. She also reflected on how difficult it was for her to stop herself (or back down, as she put it), when she had got herself dug into a conflict in this way. This parent also came to understand why mobile phones were not permitted in the nursery and decided that she did not wish to make a formal complaint after all.

My final question, as I draw to a close is:

Do you and your team exercise this kind of professional maturity in your practice and genuinely place the needs of children at the heart of everything you do?

KEY POINTS IN SYSTEMS TO SUPPORT THE WELL-BEING OF THE PROVISION

- A comprehensive and coherent approach to safeguarding children, their families and each other, as practitioners is actively reflected in daily practice. It should be noted that this is never a *done deal*, but a constantly evolving process, in which everyone is accountable

- The Designated Person for Safeguarding is essential to keeping practitioners (or family members, for home-based child care), up to date with modern practice, including key messages from Serious Case Reviews. They *must* hold a confident working knowledge of their role, have the skills to interpret, assess and analyse what they observe, hold sufficient professional authority to set and maintain standards and effect change, where necessary

References

Allen, G. (2011) *Early Intervention: The Next Steps* (http://www.education.gov.uk).

Cleaver, H., Unell, I. and Algate, J. (1999) *Children's Needs – Parenting Capacity: The impact of parental mental illness, problem alcohol and drug use, and domestic violence on children's development*, London, TSO (The Stationery Office).

CWDC (2010) *Common Core of Skills And Knowledge*, Leeds, CWDC.

CWDC (2009) *The Common Assessment Framework for Children & Young People*, Leeds, CWDC.

The CWDC transferred to the DfE on 31/3/12. Documents can be found on this website: www.education.gov.uk

Daniel B, Wassell S and Gilligan R. (2010) *Child Development for Child Care and Protection Workers* (2nd edition) London, Jessica Kingsley.

DCSF (2008) *Information Sharing: Guidance for practitioners and managers*, Nottingham, DCSF.

DfE (2012) *Statutory Framework for the Early Years Foundation Stage.*

DCSF (2010) *Working Together to Safeguard Children*, Nottingham, DCSF Publications (currently under review).

Daniel Denison, Colleen Lief and John L. Ward 'Culture in Family-Owned Enterprises: Recognizing and Leveraging Unique Strengths' DOI: 10.1111/j.1741-6248.2004.00004.x *Family Business Review* 2004; 17; 61

DfES (2006) *What to do if you're worried a child is being abused*, Nottingham, DfES.

DoH (2000) *Framework for the Assessment of Children in Need and their Families*, London, TSO.

Executive Summary in respect of Nursery Z. Plymouth, (2010) Plymouth Safeguarding Children Board.

Field, F. (2010) *The Foundation Years: preventing poor children becoming poor adults*, London, Cabinet Office.

Kolb, D.A. (1984) *Experiential Learning experience as a source of learning and development*, New Jersey, Prentice Hall.

Munro, E. (2011) *The Munro Review of Child Protection: A Child Centred System*, Norwich, TSO.

The Children Act 1989, TSO; The Children Act 2004, TSO.

The Childcare Act 2006, TSO.

Tickell, C. (2011) *The Early Years Foundation Stage (EYFS) Review* (http://www.education.gov.uk).

Women's Aid 2011 (http://www.womensaid.org.uk).

Further reading

Tassoni, P. *Practical EYFS Handbook*, Heinemann (2008).

Robinson, M. *From Birth to One: The Year of Opportunity*, OUP (2003).

Howe, D. *Child Abuse and Neglect: Attachment, Development and Intervention*, Palgrave Macmillan (2005).

Manning-Morton, J. *Key Times for Play: The First Three Years*, OUP (2003).

Gerhardt, S. *Why Love Matters: How Affection Shapes a Baby's Brain*, Routledge (2004).

Acknowledgements

There are a number of very special people to whom I wish to extend my gratitude.

Thank you to Practical Pre-School Books for inviting me to write the book in the first place. It has been a fascinating journey, with an extraordinary and unexpected outcome. 'Downloading my philosophy' for safeguarding children, their families and each other within Children's Services, has created new brain-space for a multitude of new and fresh ideas.

I thank my family and friends for being a constant source of encouragement and love. In particular my mum, who on reading the first chapters said 'It's time Cath, get on with it'. I believe that might just be our family motto, extending over many generations!

Thank you to my 'String of Pearls' friends, a group of the most inspirational individuals creating transformational projects over the world. Thank you in particular to Dominic, who I talked with early every morning, before I started writing.

My Associate Team at Catherine Rushforth and Associates has been amazing. They supported my ordering of ideas, were a constant pool of inspiration and encouragement. In particular my huge thanks to Karen Fishwick, my senior associate, who made the first edit on all the chapters and translated some of my wordy descriptions into more accessible English. Our shared values for work with the early years sector have become even more sharply refined. Karen has been like my personal doula, she was there throughout the full gestation and birthing period, reminding me when to breathe, push and rest! Thank you.

As many people will know, I have worked in Children's Services as an early years practitioner, centre manager, social worker, family therapist, trainer and consultant for over 30 years. In the early 1980s Fiona Phillips, the most extraordinarily committed woman, arrived at my early years provision. Under her leadership an unwavering expectation of sensitive, truly child-centred practice with parents as genuine partners, became the norm. I thank

Fiona for her commitment towards everyone she encounters; she exemplifies humility, grace and faith in our capacity to truly care. We have worked together for over 30 years now and she never fails to inspire and touch me deeply.

There is a huge body of early years practitioners who I meet in the course of my work. Many were right there with me, in my mind's eye, as I typed. I reflected on the challenges you have faced, the difference you make in children's lives and the ways in which you grow and evolve yourselves as 'artists in human relationships'. As I thought of you, specific managers, practitioners and teams came to mind. I wanted to publicly commend you for the great work that you do with children and their families and at long last found a way to do this – I refer to your practice in case studies, some I name and others declined being named. I applaud all of you for the heart that you bring to your work. Thank you in particular to:

- Kathy and the complete staff team at Aylesbury Early Years Centre. I was bowled over by how many of you wanted to talk with me about how you have achieved consistently warm, respectful relationships with parents, even in the most challenging of circumstances. Thank you for talking with many of the children's parents and for getting their agreement to being involved in the photoshoot. Given the subject matter of the book, their agreement is a testament to their trust in you.

- Nakissa and her practitioner team at Stars of Hope Nursery. I was struck by the warm relationships that you have established with children and parents. Their willingness to be involved indicates the honesty and openness of their relationships with you.

- Mel, Justine, Bella and Sophie at Zoom Nurseries for agreeing to be profiled in print as a 'Centre for Excellence' as a progressive learning organisation.

- Cathryn, Neil, Alan, Anita and Dave at Clyde Children's Centre for providing a tranquil working environment to write.